IMAGES OF PORTSMOUTH

IMAGES OF PORTSMOUTH

Sarah Quail and John Stedman

The Breedon Books
Publishing Company
Derby

First published in Great Britain by
The Breedon Books Publishing Company Limited
44 Friar Gate, Derby DE1 1DA
1993

ISBN 1 873626 25 8

Printed and bound by Hillmans Printers, Frome, Somerset.
Colour section printed by H.A.Smith Ltd of Coventry.
Covers printed by BDC Printing Services Ltd of Derby.

Contents

For
Anthony and Hugh
and
Janet and Sarah

Abbreviations
nd: no date
PCM: Portsmouth City Museums
PCRO: Portsmouth City Records Office
PCRO DL/P: Portsmouth City Records Office Leisure Department Collection.
PCRO CEng/P: Portsmouth City Records Office City Engineers Collection
PCRO Reprogr: Portsmouth City Records Office; original generated by staff of the Reprographic Section

Introduction

THE illustrations in this book have been selected from the collections of Portsmouth City Museums and the Portsmouth City Records Office. These collections have been assembled over some fifty years through gifts, purchases and long-term loans. The richness and variety of the collections is particularly remarkable when it is recalled that the old Borough Museum in the High Street — and its contents — was destroyed in the first full year of World War Two.

Our aim in producing the book has been to make the collections more widely known and, hence, more accessible and, in some small way, to tell people a little more about the history of Portsmouth, for these pictures are visual history. And it is well worth remembering the old adage that every picture is worth a thousand words.

Some readers may feel that we have not given due weight to Portsmouth's naval history. We must point out therefore that our collections are the *city's* records not the navy's. Whilst of course there are sections in this book devoted to the Royal Navy and the dockyard, they are only *part* of the story of Portsmouth. Comprehensive collections of photographs of naval images can be consulted in specialist institutions such as the Royal Naval Museum, Portsmouth, the Royal Marines Museum at Eastney and the National Maritime Museum at Greenwich.

Some readers may also be surprised that there is no extensive coverage of Portsmouth during World War Two. A fine archive of such photographs does exist, but it is the property of Portsmouth and Sunderland Newspapers and not Portsmouth City Council. However, that said, we have, hopefully, assembled here a collection of images that, between them, convey effectively some picture of Portsmouth's past and some record of the city today. All the pictures are available for consultation in our respective establishments.

Many people have helped us select and identify the photographs and collate them into their different categories: our colleagues in Portsmouth City Museums and the City Records Office; the staff of the Reprographic Section, Portsmouth Contract Services, who skilfully copied each picture, and the staff of Portsmouth Central Library who dealt with many queries on our behalf. To the many people who have donated pictures to us or have placed them on long-term loan in our respective institutions and thereby given us permission to publish, we extend our grateful thanks. All profits from the sale of this publication will be divided equally between Portsmouth City Museums and the City Records Office and will be used to conserve the collections.

Sarah Quail and John Stedman
April 1993

Portsmouth in Panorama

T HE MODERN city of Portsmouth occupies mainly an island site on Hampshire's southern coast. It is a densely populated area of just over four hectares with a population of approximately 184,000. Its long association with the defence of the realm and the Royal Navy has inevitably shaped its development significantly.

The town's history began in the late twelfth century when a wealthy Norman merchant and entrepreneur, Jean de Gisors, purchased the manor of Buckland in the centre of Portsea Island and with it the marshy, inhospitable spit at the harbour entrance called *Sudewede* or south water. There he set about developing a trading post. This grew quickly into a town which he named Portsmouth. A church was built, dedicated to the recently-martyred Thomas à Becket (now the Anglican Cathedral Church of St Thomas of Canterbury). A water mill was also built, a dock, at least one substantial merchant's house and houses for the ordinary townsfolk. The twelfth-century grid street plan still survives in its essentials today.

Rebellion against the English king, Richard I, cost Jean de Gisors his new town and his other lands in southern England. They were confiscated by the king. Confiscated lands were usually sold on by the Crown to the highest bidder but this did not happen in Portsmouth. The king held on to the town and Portsmouth became a royal borough. Between 1194 and his death in 1199, Richard spent a great deal of money on the town: a royal residence was built, building sites were leased to new settlers and he, too, built docking facilities. He also granted Portsmouth its first charter, in May 1194.

Richard was, without doubt, influenced by the strategic advantages of the site. He needed a reliable port on the south coast for the assembly and embarkation of troops for Normandy and his territories further south, and a great natural harbour such as Portsmouth's could not fail to be important for such purposes. Portsmouth was also a crucial link in a line of communication stretching from the old Norman administrative centre of Rouen to its fast-developing rival, Caen, and from thence across the Channel to Portsmouth and finally Winchester where the English Treasury was based.

Normandy was lost by Richard's successor, his brother John, in 1204 but money was still spent on Portsmouth in the early thirteenth century: a chapel and quarters for the queen were built on the site of the royal residence, although by the late thirteenth century these dwellings has fallen into disrepair. Whilst some hope remained of recapturing the old Norman territories, Portsmouth's continued prosperity was guaranteed but, once that hope faded, official interest in the town declined.

French raids in the late fourteenth century — as a result of the Hundred Years War — concentrated official attention on the town once more. There was an official inquiry into Portsmouth's defences and it is probable that, shortly afterwards, the land circuit of the town was fenced with a ditch and a pallisade. In 1416 work began on the Round Tower, now the oldest surviving part of the fortifications. Towards the end of the century, building started on the Square Tower and a bulwark to protect the town — and the newly-established victualling base there — on the seaward side. By the end of Henry VII's reign, Portsmouth was one of the most heavily defended areas in northern Europe.

Henry VII also built a dry dock in Portsmouth in 1495-96 — the first in Europe. He subsequently declared the town a Royal Dockyard and a Garrison Town. These were events of fundamental importance for Portsmouth's future history. The further growth of the town is the result of development of the dockyard. The Dutch Wars of the late seventeenth century, followed by a succession of wars against the French ending only in 1815, brought much work to the ever-growing dockyard and hundreds — eventually thousands — of people to the town. Houses began to be built in the early eighteenth century outside the walls of the original settlement on common fields round the dockyard which stood in the neighbouring parish of Portsea. The area was known as Portsmouth Common and it developed rapidly. By 1753 the local population was demanding a church of its own and, in due course, the new suburb was fortified and, under an Improvement Act of 1792, it became known officially as Portsea.

More development came in the late eighteenth and early nineteenth centuries. The working-class district of Landport grew up to the east of Portsea. The fashionable suburb and seaside resort of Southsea developed to the south. The town's population census figures tell the story themselves: they rose from 32,000 in 1801 to 190,000 in 1901. By the beginning of the twentieth century a series of boundary extensions had brought the whole of Portsea Island within the borough

In 1545 the English fleet engaged a French invasion fleet in the Solent as Henry VIII watched from Southsea. The battle was inconclusive although the English lost the *Mary Rose*. A mural recording the scene was painted in Cowdray House, Midhurst, and this engraving was made of the painting. Besides the battle it shows the new defences of Portsmouth and the new castle at Southsea. It is the earliest view of the town.   (PCM 248/1948)

boundaries and the commercial centre of the town had shifted northwards away from the historic old town to Landport. The opening of a splendid new town hall in Landport in 1890 (renamed the Guildhall in 1926 when Portsmouth was raised to the dignity of a city) was confirmation of this shift.

Because of changes in the range and effectiveness of artillery in the last half of the century, a new chain of forts was built on Portsdown Hill and sea forts in the Solent. The existing ramparts round Portsmouth and the suburb of Portsea were rendered redundant. During the 1870s and 1880s, they were demolished systematically with the exception of the seaward defences which still stand guard at the harbour mouth.

By 1920, the borough had spread on to mainland Hampshire and had incorporated the civil parish of Cosham. The present boundaries were established in 1932 when parts of the parishes of Portchester and Farlington were absorbed within the city. During World War Two, Portsmouth, like so many important provincial centres, was heavily bombed. Significant

swathes of the old town and the district of Landport were razed to the ground. Large numbers of the displaced population were rehoused on the mainland, often outside the city boundaries on new estates, most notably the Leigh Park Estate, built in the borough of Havant.

The Royal Navy and defence-related activities no longer play such an important role in the life of the town as they did in pre-war days. Local employment has had to diversify and develop to take account of the accelerated run-down of the dockyard since the Defence Review of 1981 and this trend will inevitably continue. However, in this very brief overview or panorama of Portsmouth's history, it is possible to identify one consistent theme or strand — the significance of the town's strategic position throughout the centuries here on England's south coast. Eight hundred years ago, ships left our shores carrying mercenary armies to France. Today a modern fleet of super ferries carries a new invading army — of tourists — to foreign shores!

Panorama of shoreline of Portsmouth from the Dockyard to Clarence Pier by Jabez Hughes of Ryde, Isle of Wight, *c*.1861. (PCRO 468A)

Portsmouth Grammar School opened in 1750 in Penny Street. In the mid-nineteenth century it decayed and was refounded in 1873. This new building, at the top of the High Street, was opened in 1879. The school has flourished and took over part of the former Clarence Barracks in 1926. (PCM 960/1974a)

In 1628 John Felton assassinated King Charles I's favourite, the Duke of Buckingham, in this house. Felton had been an officer during the duke's disastrous attempt to relieve La Rochelle in 1627. Buckingham was staying here, in the house of a prominent citizen, Captain John Mason, while preparing a new expedition against France. Now called Buckingham House, the building was joined to its neighbour and refronted about 1700, but still retains its timber-framing behind the new façade. (PCM 102/1976)

The George Hotel, in the High Street, was the most prestigious inn in Portsmouth in the eighteenth and nineteenth centuries. There Nelson ate his last meal on English soil. This engraving shows it in the late 1930s. It was destroyed in the blitz.
(PCM 416/1974)

An early photograph of the High Street, taken in 1868. The shop on the corner of Pembroke Road is a butcher's. The street is lit by gas lamps — a gas company was founded in Portsmouth in 1821.
(PCM 820/1981)

One of Edward King's wartime oil paintings of the damage done to Portsmouth during the blitz. Here the cathedral stands in the ruins of the High Street. On the right can be seen the pediment of the museum, formerly the town hall, a victim of the bombing.
(PCM 460/1945)

The southern end of the High Street, about 1880. Grand Parade is on the right. The houses on the left-hand side of the street stand in front of St Thomas' church. Tramlines run down the street — these were for a service from Point to North End begun in 1874.
(PCM)

Portsmouth's Anglican Cathedral and the Power Station, *c.*1960. The ancient parish church of St Thomas of Canterbury became the cathedral church of the newly-created Anglican diocese of Portsmouth in 1927. It was partially extended in 1938-9 by Sir Charles Nicholson. The outbreak of war in 1939 brought works to an abrupt conclusion and a temporary brick wall was erected. A new scheme for completing the building was brought to a successful conclusion 1989-92 to designs of architect Michael Drury. The first plant at Portsmouth Power Station was commissioned in 1894. The site was cleared for residential devdelopment in the early 1980s. (PCRO 418A/4/3)

Grand Parade, 1870. On the left is the guardhouse for the soldiers manning the ramparts and gates. The memorial is to the soldiers of the 8th (King's) Regiment. (PCM 938/1974)

The novelist, George Meredith, was born above this, his father's house in the High Street, on 12 February 1828. The photograph was taken *c*.1930. The house was destroyed in the blitz.   (**PCRO** 540A/1/12)

Aerial view of Old Portsmouth, *c.*1930, from above the Victoria Pier, the former beef landing stage, adjoining the Square Tower. In 1842 the old landing stage had been transformed into the Victoria Pier. Although used mainly as a landing place for steamer passengers, it became a popular resort of local residents. (PCRO 839A/1)

Portsmouth and South Hampshire Eye and Ear Infirmary, nd. Opened 1884, it stood at the corner of Clarence View and Pembroke Road. (PCRO 1499A/16)

Pembroke Road in 1870, after the demolition of King William's Gate. On the right can be seen the Royal Naval Club, before its tower was built. On the left of the road is the guardhouse, which still stands.   (PCM 420/1981)

Owen Tottye's house, King Street. Tottye was a leading merchant, and several times mayor of Portsmouth. He died in 1602. The picture was painted by R.H.C.Ubsdell, probably just before the building was demolished in the mid-nineteenth century.
(PCM 105/1964)

Old properties in Oyster Street, Old Portsmouth, *c.*1930.

(PCRO 540A/1/7)

Old wooden houses in St Thomas' Street, *c.*1930.

(PCRO 540A/1/9)

King James' Gate divided the respectable townsfolk of Old Portsmouth from the disreputable establishments on Point patronised by sailors on leave. The two buildings on the left of this early nineteenth-century print are pubs, typical of the many drinking houses, brothels, cookshops and retailers of cheap clothing to be found in the area in the eighteenth and early nineteenth centuries. (PCM 108/1958)

The west side of Broad Street, Point, probably about 1840. This row of buildings was demolished in 1847 when the Point Artillery Barracks were put up. On the left is the Sally Port; to its left was the moat in front of King James' Gate. The four buildings closest to the Sally Port are pubs. (PCM 18p/1988)

Pipers Alley, Point, 1935. R.Grassey's gouache vividly demonstrates the cramped and humble housing which characterised Point.
(PCM 574/1964)

Bath Square, Point, *c.*1900. In 1754 a 'commodious bathinghouse' (now Quebec House) was erected by public subscription on the seaward side of the square. It had four baths in its basement, filled at high tide by the sea. At this date sea bathing was becoming popular as a medical treatment and as a recreation. (PCM H/82/52)

Portsmouth Point and the *Still and West Country House* in its pre-World War II run-down state. (PCRO DL/P)

Portsmouth Point, Oct 26 1830, a pen and ink wash drawing by Capt. E.W.Harrington, RN. Most of the buildings on the northern end of Point were warehouses or workshops at this date. In 1840 the terminus of the Floating Bridge to Gosport was constructed more-or-less where the lamp-post stands. The slipway formerly at the end of Broad Street was just to the right of the man with the wheelbarrow.   (PCM 34/1956)

Camber showing *Orange Tree Tavern,* nd.*c.*1880.   (PCRO 1499A/26)

The Camber, *c*.1930. To the left of the *Bridge Tavern* are unloading gantries and storage facilities for the large quantities of coal that came into Portsmouth by sea.

(PCM 752/1964)

The Camber, Portsmouth, about 1915. This etching by G.A.Horne shows the bascule bridge which spanned the Camber between 1842 and about 1916.

(PCM 21/1951b)

Unloading timber from Finland on the quayside opposite Custom House. Outer Camber, 1928. H.E. Young's watercolour
shows one of the many sailing vessels which still used the harbour at this time. (PCM 227/1981)

The Camber, *c*.1930.

(PCRO 1518A/1/24)

John Pounds (1766-1839) was the inspiration of the Ragged Schools movement. Pounds was apprenticed in the Dockyard, but was crippled in an accident and forced to earn a meagre living as a cobbler. There was then little schooling for the children of the poor, so he began teaching street urchins the three R's as he worked. By his death he had taught hundreds. His small shop, with a living-room-cum-bedroom above, stood in Highbury Street.

(PCM 1084/1980)

This engraving of the Dockyard gate and *The Navy Tavern* was published in 1833 as an advertisement for the sale of the pub. Many of the buildings on The Hard were drinking houses. (PCM 9/1949)

The Common Hard, just outside the main gate to the Dockyard, provided public access to the harbour. This photograph, which was taken about 1895, shows that graffiti is not a modern problem. (PCM 946/1974)

The Hard, Portsea, *c.*1910. The first houses appeared on Ship and Castle Row, later The Hard, *c.*1708. By the late eighteenth century there were 35 businesses listed in contemporary directories of which 13 were inns. At the main entrance to the Dockyard, The Hard enjoyed an unenviable reputation. In 1859, law-abiding local residents petitioned the Town Council for better police protection declaring that drunken men and prostitutes were permitted, without molestation, to infest the place at all hours of the day, and when a ship happened to pay off, 'the Hard presents a scene of drunkeness and profigacy which baffles all description'.   (PCRO215A/3/5)

Marines marching out of the Dockyard's main gate and along the Hard, possibly after disembarking, nd.   (PCRO DL/P)

Queen Street *en fête*, possibly in 1905. Almost every building is Georgian in date.   (PCM 227/1979)

Queen Street at the junction with Lion Terrace, *c.*1910. The postcard demonstrates the narrowness of the street as it was first laid out. It was substantially widened after 1945.   (Hants County Libraries Portsmouth)

Housing opposite the Dockyard wall, Portsea, painted *c.*1810. These were some of the better-quality homes in Portsea.

(PCM 109/1964)

The Inn of Good Fellowship, Kent Street, *c.*1920. Attached to the Kent Street Baptist Church, the *Inn of Good Fellowship* was a temperance venture where the needy could secure a bowl of soup and be sure of a welcome. Kent Street Baptist Church is to the left, set back.

(PCRO 477A/4/47)

Early eighteenth-century cottages in Kent Street. Portsea was developed piecemeal to provide homes for workmen from the Dockyard. The first houses there were built in the 1690s. **(PCM 657/1974)**

Houses in Cross Street and Butchers Street, 1894, fairly representative of the smaller eighteenth-century homes and shops in Portsea. **(PCM H/71/94)**

Bateman's Alley was typical of the many slum courts in Portsea which had grown up by 1850. Houses in these places were small, badly ventilated, often overshadowed by surrounding buildings and had poor sanitation and water supplies. There was no room, or money, to build anything better inside the ramparts.

(PCM H/71/94)

A street in Portsea, painted by E.A.Phipson between 1890 and 1894. These houses were built for better-off craftsmen in the town during the first half of the eighteenth century. Unlike the many humbler houses they had small front gardens, but the elaborate doorcases were almost universal.

(PCM 18/1950)

The Marlborough Gate. Not so well known as Main Gate or Unicorn Gate, the Marlborough Gate stood at the top of Marlborough Row, Portsea.   (PCRO 1201A/4/1)

Landport and Neighbours

This aerial photograph taken in the 1930s demonstrates clearly the character of so much of the Victorian housing of Portsea Island. The gridiron streetplan of the areas of working-class housing in Somerstown and northern Southsea contrast strikingly with the curving, tree-lined streets of Thomas Ellis Owen's Southsea, off the picture to the left.

(PCM 642/1974)

Ivy Street, Somerstown, looking towards Somerville Road, 1962. (PCRO CEng/PG 31a)

Rear views of 23-38 Henrietta Street, Landport, 1961-2. In the background is the spire of the *Mystery* public house, 1-3 Warwick Street. (PCRO CEng/PG 30)

Rear of properties situated on the south side of Henrietta Street, Landport, 1961.　　　　(PCRO CEng/PG 26)

Royal Marines Orphan School and Female Orphan Home shortly before it was demolished in 1967 to make way for a new road. Built in 1874, this building replaced their former premises in Lion Terrace, Portsea.　　　(PCRO 827A/15/34/1)

Albertolli's Continental Café-Restaurant, 63-65, Commercial Road, *c.*1937.

(PCRO 972A/1/3)

The Guildhall and Guildhall Square, pre-1939. The new Town Hall in Landport, known as the Guildhall after 1926 when Portsmouth became a city, was opened in 1890 replacing the more modest building in the High Street opened in 1838 which became the Borough Museum. The move reflected the shift which had taken place as the town's business community quit the old commercial centre of the High Street for the new burgeoning suburb of Landport. It is no coincidence that Landport's main throroughfare now became Commercial Road. The Municipal College behind the Guildhall opened in 1908.

(PCRO 1518A/1/43)

Portsmouth from the Town Hall clock face looking over towards Russell Street and into Eldon Street, 1906.
(PCRO 477A/3/14)

Portsmouth from the Town Hall clock face looking towards the *Central Hotel* in Commercial Road, 1906.

(PCRO 477A/3/15)

The Town Hall Square, *c.*1910, looking south down Commercial Road.

(PCRO 946A/8)

Russell Street at the junction with Swan Street, c.1930. Russell Street opened into Guildhall Square and was demolished when the new civic offices and library were built.   **(PCM 657/1974)**

Greetham Street from the steps of the Town Hall, c.1930. Horse-drawn vehicles are still more common than motor vehicles. The railway goods sheds and yard occupy the left background.   **(PCM 472/1974)**

Looking northwards under the railway bridge from Guildhall Square, 1899. This bridge was constructed in 1876 when the railway was extended to the harbour.

(PCM 942/1974b)

An unusual view of Guildhall Square, taken from the roof of the Guildhall *c.*1910. The statue of Queen Victoria was erected in 1903.

(PCM 656/1945r)

Commerical Road at the junction with Edinburgh Road, about 1895. The Landport Drapery Bazaar stood on the corner of Arundel Street, where Allders is today.

(PCM 947/1974)

The Cascades Centre was opened in September 1989. An attractive, large indoor shopping mall with car parking above, it is an example of a national trend in retailing development.

(PCRO Reprogr)

The headquarters of the Zurich Insurance Co stands beside Victoria Park. It is arguably Portsmouth's most impressive modern building, finished in 1977.

(PCRO Reprogr)

Commercial Road at the junction with Arundel Street, *c*.1930. The 1977 Jubilee memorial fountain occupies this spot now. The Landport Drapery Bazaar, on the right, was bombed in 1941.
(PCM 187/1976)

Commercial Road at the Lake Road junction, looking north, *c*.1900. It is market day and the wagons and carts of carriers from the surrounding rural districts fill the streets.
(PCM 468/1974)

Commercial Road near Charlotte Street *c*.1905, lined with wagons on market day. Portsmouth Corporation Tramways car 26 threads its way through the traffic.

(PCM)

Commercial Road, post World War II, looking south. Samuel's is still on the same spot.   (PCRO DL/P)

The Portsea Island General Cemetery was at Mile End, Rudmore. After it became disused the frontage was let out as
a petrol station. The site became a park and is now parking space for the ferryport.   (PCM 129/1945)

Charles Dickens' birthplace. The novelist was born in Mile End Terrace on 8 February 1812. The building, now one of the city's Museums, has survived remarkably unscathed. (PCRO 694A/9/1/80)

Ashford House, 401 Commercial Road, Portsmouth, 1958. The old Mile End Cemetery and a number of handsome early-nineteenth century villas and terraces once stood in Mile End on land occupied today by the Continental Ferry Port, dual carriageways and post-war council housing. (PCRO 722A/5/10/4/3/1)

A watercolour of Rudmore Windmill, which stood just north of the modern ferryport. Behind is a bottle-shaped kiln, probably for drying corn before milling.

(PCM 82/1962)

London Road, North End, early 1950s.   (PCRO 348A/1/1/4)

The funeral procession of a Portsmouth Corporation Tramways employee in Chichester Road, Kingston, *c.*1920. There is a horse-drawn hearse and coach in the middle of the procession, and a band.   (PCM 48/1980)

Newspaper boys outside J.Hales' shop on the corner of Newcomen Road and Twyford Avenue, *c.*1905. This shop is still a newsagent's.   (PCM H/74/20)

Chichester Road, North End, *c.*1910. Development began here in 1879.   (PCRO 687A/1/9/31)

London Road, North End, *c*.1910. Again, development began spreading north along what is now London Road in the 1870s.
(PCRO 151A/7/91)

London Road at the junction with Gladys Avenue *c*.1923. The corporation's transport depot was just up Gladys Avenue. White's furniture repository can be seen on the right.
(PCM 604/1974)

A similar view seven or eight years later. Percy Tuck, a newsagent, was in business for most of the 1920s and '30s. The new building at the junction is Southdown Buildings, occupied by the bus company. (PCM 788/1980)

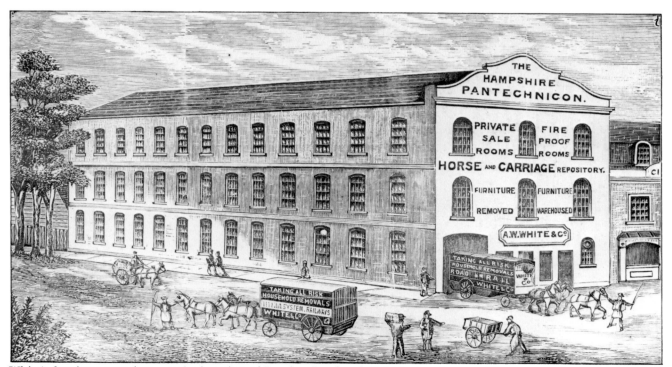

White's furniture repository, at the junction of London Road and Stubbington Avenue. The company's offices were sited in the more prestigious location of Cambridge Junction, at the top of Old Portsmouth High Street. From a guide book to Southsea published in 1889. (PCM)

Tramcar 114 being towed into North End tram depot in Gladys Avenue, 1920, by a Colyer & Co lorry. It would have arrived at Cosham by rail. Behind the lorry can be seen the gates to the depot, now outside the City Museum. (PCM H/66/92)

North End Swimming Pond, *c.*1910. The pond stood at the bottom of Strode Road and Gruneison Road, Stamshaw.
(PCRO 1433A/12/30/2/25)

London Road, Hilsea, *c*.1910. Taken near the entrance to the Artillery Barracks built at Hilsea in 1854. (PCRO 708A/2/18)

A series of temporary barracks stood at Hilsea from the reign of George II. In 1854 a permanent barracks was built for the Royal Artillery. The Ridings now runs across the site. (PCM 1073/1980)

Winston Churchill, First Lord of the Admiralty, flies into Hilsea Drill field and is received by Royal Field Artillery officers, May 1914.
(PCRO 494A.45)

Green Farm, Hilsea, painted by E.A.Phipson in 1894. This is reputed to have been the last working commercial farm on Portsea Island. The farmhouse, which has a thatched roof and is of timber-frame construction, is seventeenth century, while the taller extension with the slate roof is nineteenth century. The clapboard building on the left, with the pyramidical roof is a granary.
(PCM 18/1950)

The Children's Bathing Pool at Hilsea in the 1930s.   (PCRO DL/P)

Tipner Magazine, from a wash drawing of about 1858. There was a magazine at Tipner, well away from habitation, from before 1801, although the present magazines may date from 1830.   (PCM 1117/1973)

Cottages at Hilsea, *c.*1920. A good example of the local vernacular architecture. Demolished in the 1930s.   (PCRO)

The barn at Great Salterns. It is said to have been used to store salt made in the local saltpans. There were saltpans on Portsea Island in 1086.
                                                                                          (PCM 452/1974)

Stubbington Avenue, 1929. This road was one of those laid out during the Edwardian period, as the style of its substantial houses indicates. The area had been farmland — Stubbington Lodge stood roughly where the Church of the Ascension now stands.

(PCM 648/1974)

The *Black Prince* public house, 68 Upper Arundel Street, Portsmouth, 1939.   (PCRO 114A/C2/13/2/2/1)

Portsea Parish Institute, Fratton Road, from the tower of St Mary's Portsea, pre-1939. Designed by Sir Reginald Blomfield in 1899, it was the first home of the Northern Secondary School 1921-32. In recent years the building has been the home of Radio Victory and, currently, Portsmouth Housing Association.

(PCRO 1393A/9/1)

The annual May Day procession passing through Fratton *c*.1890. Firemen are in the lead, the corporation's horses, with elaborate decoration, are following them. May Day, a traditional festival, was celebrated in style in Victorian and Edwardian Portsmouth. From a drawing by H.Coish. (PCM H/71/94)

Fratton Road, *c*.1910. (PCM 308/1979)

The ceremony marking the widening of Fratton Road, 1929. Portsmouth's principal roads in 1900 followed the lin

country lanes. They were not adequate for the growing motor traffic of the twentieth century. (PCM 661/1974)

Charles Simmonds' beer shop stood at 90-92 Byerley Road. It is typical of hundreds of similar beer shops which provided a home from home for the men folk of the families who lived in the adjacent densely populated streets. Byerley Road runs from the entrance of Kingston Recreation Ground to Walmer Road.   (PCRO 1389A/1/15)

St Mary's Church from the south. The railway cutting runs across the foreground of this drawing by H. Coish. It is clear how the church towered above all the neighbouring buildings, having cathedral-like proportions.   (PCM H/71/94)

Copnor Road, *c.*1930. These houses were built in 1928.

(PCM 59/1992)

Portsmouth Brickworks between the wars. The brickworks covered the Burrfields Road industrial estate area. Much of Portsea Island is brickearth and before this brickworks was established most of the bricks needed to build Portsmouth's houses were fired near the construction site in 'clamps', the clay being dug on site.

(PCM 38/1979)

The first St James' church, Milton, was consecrated in 1841. It was built in the Romansesque style to the designs of Augustus Livesay, a local architect. Local people called it the 'runaway church' because people came from other places to be married in it, and some were assumed to be eloping. It was demolished in 1913.   (PCM 427/1970)

Cottages in Milton engraved c.1915. They stood just behind the site of the present library.   (PCM 21/1951)

The old post office, Milton, at the end of the nineteenth century. The present post office is a classic 1930s building.

(PCM 914/1980)

Milton Park, pre-1914. It was purchased in 1911 when the death of local farmer and recluse James Goldsmith brought a large wooded area on to the market for development. The Town Council acquired the property for £28,840 as well as some additional land in Bransbury Road and converted their purchase to recreational use.

(PCRO 1271A/1)

The Borough Asylum, Milton, *c.*1910. It was opened in 1879 at a cost of £141,000. Until 1862 Portsmouth lunatics were sent to Knowle Asylum and thereafter to Fisherton, near Salisbury. The building and grounds at Milton originally covered an area of 75 acres.   **(PCRO 824A/2/1/8)**

St James' Hospital was opened in 1879 as a lunatic asylum. Its grounds were extensive and until 1965 patients contributed to their keep by cultivating them. Changes in the name of the hospital reflected changes in Society's view of mental illness: The Borough of Portsmouth Lunatic Asylum; Portsmouth Borough Mental Hospital (1920); St James' Hospital for Nervous and Mental Diseases (1937); St James' Psychiatric Hospital (1960). This postcard shows the hospital about 1960.   **(PCM 132/1985/1)**

Sewage-storage tanks under construction just north of Fort Cumberland, 1886. By 1880 the mains drainage scheme of 1865-7 needed improving to stop sewage being washed back on to Eastney beach. In 1886-7 new pumping engines were installed (in what is now Eastney Industrial Museum) and these reservoirs built so that all the city's sewage could be released out to sea in the first hours of the ebb tide. (PCM M/3603)

Eastney Barracks was built to house the Royal Marine Artillery, which had occupied barracks in Fort Cumberland since 1858. They took the new barracks over in 1860. The Royal Marine Light Infantry, whose base had been moved to Gosport in 1848, returned to Portsmouth and was amalgamated with the RMA to form the Royal Marines in 1923. The ramparts of the fort originally on this site can be seen in the foreground. (PCM 8873/10)

Adair Road, Eastney, nd. Milk deliveries! Constructed *c.*1896, Adair Road is one of a number of densely-populated streets which developed in the vicinity of the Marines Barracks in the years following their construction.   (PCRO Reprogr.1950)

King's Terrace with its adjacent terrace, Jubilee Terrace, *c.*1830. Built during the Regency, King's and Jubilee Terraces honour George III. Amongst the earliest Southsea development, they follow the outer boundary of Portsmouth's fortifications facing westwards over the open ground of the glacis to the ramparts of the old town. A contemporary writer once compared the vista to a gentleman's park! There are certainly cattle grazing in the foreground. King's Terrace was destroyed but for the central section beneath the pediment during World War Two. (PCRO 857A p.397)

King's, Jubilee and Bellevue Terraces, 1847. In the distance are Hampshire and Landport Terraces with St Paul's Church, 1822, rising behind. In the foreground, the townsfolk are enjoying the recreational facility afforded them by the grassy, open space of the glacis. (PCRO 857A p.295)

Bellevue Terrace and the *Pier Hotel* with the Fitzclarence Monument, 1875. The *Pier Hotel* opened in 1865. 'Bleak and bulky' and 'a typical mid-Victorian seaside hotel' according to the 'Hampshire' volume in the *Penguin Buildings of England* series. It had nevertheless sixty bedrooms, coffee-, billiard- and dining-rooms. Today it is University of Portsmouth undergraduate accommodation. The column honoured Lord Frederick Fitzclarence, who became Governor of Portsmouth in 1847 and gave his support to the scheme for building a promenade along the seafront. The column was erected in 1852 at a cost of slightly less than the grant of £387 10s from the Treasury towards the building of the Clarence Esplanade, as it was named.   (PCRO 738A/1)

On the left is *The Five Cricketers*, which stood on the site of the *Grosvenor Hotel* at the southern end of Western Parade and was reputed to have been a smugglers' haunt in the eighteenth century. On the right is Queen's Terrace, in Kent Road. These houses, built between 1837 and 1840, were Thomas Ellis Owen's first major project in Southsea. An engraving of c.1845.   (PCM 636/1964)

Southsea Castle from the town ramparts, c.1850. The building in the centre of the picture is presumably *The Five Cricketers*. The common was a popular place of amusement. It was levelled between 1831 and 1843.   (PCM 319/1970)

St Jude's church was built in 1851 by Thomas Ellis Owen (1804-62), largely from his own pocket, as the centre-piece of his developments in Southsea. Its spire has become an important landmark for mariners. The existence of the church is at present threatened.

(PCM 1411/1974)

St Jude's Parsonage, built in 1851, drawn in 1870 looking northwards up Grove Road South. The street is broad and lined with trees, in contrast to the unrelieved lines of terraced houses typical of poorer districts.

(PCM 37p/1988)

Palmerston Road, February 1870. Although it was now possible to make larger sheets of glass than ever before, the single-sheet plate-glass windows characteristic of modern shops were still to come.

(PCM 37p/1988)

An early view of Palmerston Road at its junction with Stanley Street, *c*.1880. By at least 1860, Palmerston Road was established as the most fashionable shopping street in Southsea. Totally destroyed during World War Two, only St Jude's Church and Vicarage survive. (PCRO 1079A/1/3)

Portland Terrace, 1852. The most monumental of builder and developer Thomas Ellis Owen's Southsea terraces, Portland Terrace has definite overtones of Nash's Regents Park. Twice mayor of Portsmouth, Thomas Ellis Owen's entrepreneurial flair probably contributed most to the original, stylish mid nineteenth-century development of Southsea. Most of his terraces and many of his villas survive today and still contribute substantially to the quality of Southsea's streetscape. (PCRO 857A p.227)

No. 2 St Jude's Close, built by Thomas Ellis Owen in 1858 in a mock-Tudor style. Owen, like many other Victorian architects, sometimes indulged himself in architectural fantasy.

(PCM 147/1976)

Netley Terrace, south of Osborne Road, was completed in stages between 1859 and 1860. Although Italianate in style like most of Owen's work, it is likely that this terrace was designed by Henry Francis Gauntlett, another local architect and builder. (PCM 144/1976)

Elm Grove, 1899. Elm Grove developed as a street of large houses with big gardens for the middle classes. It got its shops only in this century. (PCM 966/1974c)

Elm Grove on a summer's day in the 1920s.

In contrast to Elm Grove, Kings Road had become an important shopping centre by 1899. H.G.Wells was apprenticed for an unhappy two years to a draper in this street in 1882-4.

(PCM 961/1974d)

Kings Road was devastated during World War Two. Here it is seen looking east from the junction with Kings Terrace, painted by Edward King not long after it was bombed. The spire in the distance belonged to Kings Road Baptist Church.

(PCM 445/1945)

Osborne Road, Southsea, *c*.1905. The awnings imply that it is a hot day. The ladies wear elaborate blouses and big hats — typical Edwardian fashion. The men and boys wear dark suits and caps in spite of the heat. (PCM)

Osborne Road at its junction with Palmerston Road, *c*.1930. (PCRO DL/P)

A lady cyclist on Clarence Parade at the junction with Lennox Road, 1899. It is remarkable that she was able to pedal with such a tight corset.   (PCM 961/1974b)

Clarence Parade at the junction with Lennox Road, c.1899. Note the invalid chair and early push-chair.   (PCM 952/1974)

The launch of the lifeboat from the Clarence Esplanade, Southsea, *c.*1900. (PCM 721/1976)

Stafford Road, Southsea, *c.*1910. The view has not altered a great deal in the last eighty years. The bathchair in the foreground is a rare detail.
(PCRO 941A/11/9)

The Dock Mill, Napier Road, Southsea, nd. Only the cottages survive today of what was an early dockyard workers' co-operative movement which pre-dated by some years the Toad Lane, Rochdale experiment of 1844. In the early 1790s a group of dockyard workers set about obtaining the means to provide their members with cheap food and drink. A windmill, a bakery and a brewery were acquired. The project had a chequered history. The Dock Mill Society and Bread Company was established in 1814. In the middle of the century it certainly had some retail outlets but very little else is known of the endeavour.   (PCRO 370A)

Napier Road, *c.*1910. This view is taken to the south of Dock Mill cottages.   (PCRO 946A/24)

Francis Avenue, Southsea, *c.*1910. Developed as part of a remarkable upsurge of building activity between 1885 and 1900, which saw field after field between Fawcett Road and the Southsea Railway covered with row upon row of houses, the Francis Avenue properties are deceptively spacious and comparatively substantial in comparison with what have been described as the bleak gridirons of artisan housing to the sides and to the north.   (PCRO 849A/23)

The Royal Clarence Promenade Rooms were created by a Mr Hollingsworth in 1824-5 on the site of a pump-room, reading-room and baths erected in 1817. They stood on the site of the future *Esplanade Hotel*. This engraving shows the interior of the assembly rooms not long after they were opened. (PCM 152/1957)

The exterior of Hollingsworth's rooms, *c.* 1830 when they became known as the King's Rooms. Bathing machines stand on the beach. In the background can be seen King's Terrace, Bellevue Terrace and the first houses in Southsea Terrace, with St Paul's church, completed 1822, peeping over the roofs. (PCM 70/1985/15)

Clarence Pier was built in 1861 to serve steamers running to the Isle of Wight. It was a short, T-shaped structure. A connection to the railway station by horse-drawn tram was opened in 1865. The pier soon became a popular promenade and very profitable to the company which owned it. The photograph shows it in 1867. (PCM 420/1981)

Clarence Pier, c.1900. Opened originally in 1861, the Clarence Pier carried the through traffic for the Isle of Wight until the completion of Portsmouth Harbour Station in 1876. A series of enlargements and improvements took place between 1869 and 1875 culminating in the opening of the pavilion in 1882. (PCRO 17A/3/4)

Donkey rides were popular in Victorian holiday resorts. In the background can be seen the pavilion on the Clarence Pier, erected in 1882, and the Southsea Rooms and Baths, built in 1870 and converted into the *Esplanade Hotel* in 1877.
(PCM 955/1974)

Southsea beach and the Clarence Esplanade, 1877. The esplanade was constructed in 1848. It was named after William IV, whose illegitimate son, Lord Frederick Fitzclarence, was Lieutenant-Governor of Portsmouth and encouraged and supported its creation.
(PCM 1404/1974)

Clarence Esplanade, *c.*1900.   (PCRO 17A/3/3/7)

Boats for hire drawn up on Southsea Beach, *c.*1895. There is a row of bathing machines on the right.   (PCM 954/1974)

Sir Thomas Lipton's *Shamrock IV*. The 1890s saw some epic struggles between yachts such as *Shamrock IV*, the Prince of Wales' *Britannia* and *Meteor*, owned by the Kaiser, in such races as the Royal Albert Yacht Club's Gold Challenge Cup.

(PCRO 494A/65)

The beach east of South Parade Pier, *c.* 1910. Bathing machines and boaters — although the beach is popular only the swimmers and paddlers are exposing their limbs. Eastney Barracks and the earthworks of Lumps Fort are visible on the skyline.
(PCM)

The Portsmouth Swimming Club diving stage near the Clarence Esplanade in 1938. In this photograph only four adults and two children are fully dressed.
(PCM 153/1976)

The Beach near the Canoe Lake, late 1940s-early 1950s. The resort emerged from the traumas of the war years to enjoy a flourishing decade of activity before package tours to Spanish resorts and cheap charter flights to the sun took their toll of the traditional seaside trade.   (PCRO DL/P)

Childrens' Paddling Pool to the west of Southsea Castle, c.1950. Built in 1928 as part of a programme of improvements and new features for Southsea Common, the paddling pool survived until the mid-1980s when the site was eventually made over to the Sealife Centre.   (PCRO DL/P)

The Rock Gardens, *c.*1950. Constructed in the late twenties the Rock Gardens, said the author of *Records of the Corporation,* 'will provide shelter from the cold winds which are occasionally felt in all seaside resorts. An interesting feature is the construction of aviaries in the rock backs so that bird lovers will be enabled to study and admire the gaily plumaged birds of foreign origin, as well as to enjoy the sweet cadence of the birds of our native land which frequent the gardens.' The Rock Gardens are still a much-loved seafront feature although the birds have long-since flown their nests!

(PCRO DL/P)

The Model Village, Lumps Fort, late 1950s. A defensive position since the sixteenth century and heavily fortified in the mid-nineteenth century, Lumps Fort was purchased by the Corporation in 1932 to prevent it becoming the site of a fun fair. It has been used for recreational purposes since World War Two.

(PCRO DL/P)

The bandstand on Southsea Common in the 1920s. Band concerts were a popular form of entertainment at this period. The apron between the deckchairs and the bandstand was used for dancing. The area is now given over to facilities for skateboard users.
(PCM)

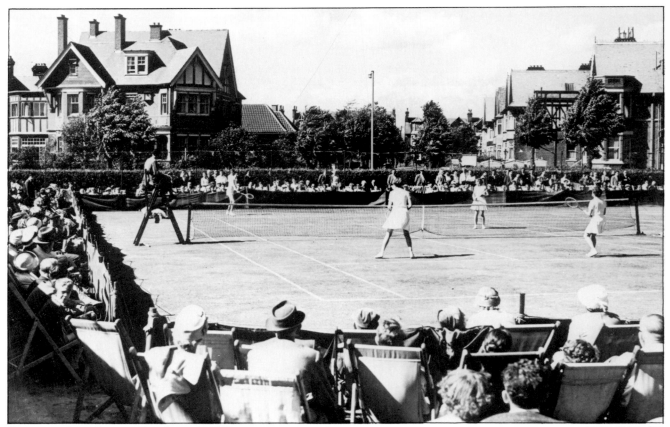

Lawn tennis on Eastern Parade, early 1950s.
(PCRO DL/P)

Canoe Lake was opened in 1886, after conversion by the town council from a 'rubbish-filled depression'. For many years competitions for model boat sailing were held here. It was also used for rowing boats and pedaloes. Elaborate water carnivals, with gondolas, were held here before 1939.   (The Trustees of the Imperial War Museum Q41369 PCM 42p/1988)

Mainland Portsmouth

The level crossing at Cosham, *c.*1900. Cosham Station was operated jointly by the London and South Western and London, Brighton and South Coast railways from its opening in 1848.
(PCM 934/1980)

From Cosham Railway Crossing *c.*1910. In the background are Queen Alexandra Hospital and, on the hill, Fort Widley.
(PCRO 708A/2/15)

Cosham High Street, from a postcard sent in 1905. Several cows share the road with cyclists and a horse-drawn vehicle.
(PCM 927/1980)

Cosham High Street, looking south, *c.*1900.

(PCRO 88A)

Cosham High Street at its junction with Havant Road, *c.*1910.

(PCRO 708A/1/5)

Havant Road, Cosham, *c.*1900. (PCRO 708A/3/12)

The fair on Portsdown Hill. Since Cosham is quite densely developed and the council's housing estate at Wymering (known as Wymering Garden City) looks well advanced, this photograph was probably taken about 1933. (PCM 607/1974)

In 1936 the D'Arcy Exploration Company began an attempt to find oil under Portsdown Hill. It was unsuccessful and they gave up in February 1938.

(PCM 620/1945)

Jones' Tea Gardens were sited in a chalk pit, almost certainly that beside the London Road immediately below the summit of Portsdown Hill. This postcard was sent as a birthday card in 1905.   (PCM)

Alexandra Military Hospital on the southern slopes of Portsdown Hill, occupied in 1908. It was built at the expense of the Admiralty in substitution for the military hospital in Lion Terrace, Portsea, which was required for the officers' quarters of the new Naval Barracks although in the end there was a change of plan and the officers' quarters were built with a frontage on to Edinburgh Road. On the skyline is Fort Widley, one of Lord Palmerston's hill forts or 'follies' built to withstand attack from the north and part of a ring of similar forts constructed around Portsmouth in the mid-nineteenth century.   (PCRO 1083A)

The gateway of Queen Alexandra Hospital. The first civilian patients were admitted in 1941. PCM 1064/1980d).

Wymering Manor. In 1859 George Nugee became Vicar of Wymering and moved into the Manor. He established a monastic community in Cosham, the Priory of St Augustine, which moved into the Manor with him. This photograph shows Gothic-style windows in what was presumably the chapel of this community. In the group are the former mayor, R.W.Ford, and his wife. The clergyman is presumably Nugee and the woman with a cross on her chest was probably a member of the female religious order, the Community of St Mary the Virgin, which Nugee installed in the vicarage. Nugee and his communities were forced to leave the parish in 1872. (PCM 660/1974)

East Wymering Farm, photographed *c*.1900. In 1935 the City and the Voluntary Association for the Blind opened it as the Jubilee Home for the Blind. It housed 26 people. It is now a home for the elderly. (PCM 665/1974)

Paulsgrove House shortly before it was demolished to make way for the M27, *c*.1970. (PCRO 320A/1/1)

Brookside Road, Bedhampton, *c.*1910. Bedhampton is approximately a mile west of Havant and perhaps two miles east of Farlington. Strictly speaking it is not within Portsmouth's boundaries although it is very much in the Portsmouth 'travel-to-work' area today.

(PCRO 1232A/2)

St Thomas' Church and the Manor House, Bedhampton, *c.*1910.

(PCRO 1232A/3)

The Elms, Bedhampton, *c.*1910. With its Gothic façade, The Elms is a most unusual house. It has a splendid Georgian reception room where the Duke of Wellington is reputed to have been entertained after Waterloo.   (PCRO 1232A/4)

Suburban development at Cosham in the late 1930s. G.& W.Mitchell began building the distinctive Highbury Estate — Hawthorn Crescent, Chatsworth Avenue and Highbury Grove — in about 1933. The houses were built in short terraces; end-of-terrace houses cost £640, those in the middle, £595. The estate proved very popular and construction was halted only by the war.   (PCM 183/1992)

The *Old House at Home*, Jubilee Avenue, Cosham. Built *c*.1946, *The Old House at Home* belonged to Portsmouth, Brighton and United Breweries Ltd, which was acquired by Brickwood & Co. Ltd in 1953. (PCRO 114A)

IBM's United Kingdom headquarters at Northarbour, Portsmouth, built on land reclaimed from the harbour, 1983. (PCRO Reprogr.169/83/A12)

Port Solent, Portsmouth's flagship marina development on reclaimed land in the northern-most reaches of Portsmouth Harbour, 1989.   (PCRO Reprogr. 96/89/B12)

The Harbour

Here and on the following pages are six panoramas of Portsmouth Harbour at the launch of HMS *Canada*, 26 August 1881, showing also HMS *St Vincent*, HMS *Victory*, HMS *Inflexible*, HMS *Assistance*, HMS *Glatton*, HMS *Wellington*, a brigantine called *Martin*, an Indian troop ship, *Serapis*, and HM yachts *Victoria and Albert II* and *Royal George*.

(PCRO 909A)

Prison hulks in Portsmouth Harbour, *c.*1810, by Louis Garneray. Hulks were used during the eighteenth and nineteenth centuries to house prisoners of war and convicts. Other PoWs. were housed in Portchester Castle. Garneray was a sailor, captured by the British in 1806 and not released until 1814. He then became a professional painter. Prisoners made many things to make a little money, including straw marquetry and bone models. Garneray painted.

(PCM 439/1970)

The prison hulk *York*, *c*.1840. An engraving by E.W.Cooke.   (**PCM** 1367/1974)

Hulks were used for several purposes besides housing prisoners, for example for storing gunpowder well away from other vessels. This engraving shows a sheer hulk, *c*.1840. It was fitted with a pair of sheerlegs to lift the heavy lower sections of ships' masts in and out of position.

(**PCM** 717/1972)

Outmoded sailing ships, including HMS *Victory* and HMS *Wellington*, provided facilities for the Navy long after their active life was over. In the background is a white-painted troopship. A watercolour by W.E.Atkins, *c*.1880. (PCM 78/1946)

Hulks in Portsmouth Harbour, 1894. A watercolour by Martin Snape. At this date hulks provided barracks for sailors and accommodated the torpedo school, HMS *Vernon*. Convicts were no longer imprisoned on hulks after 1850.

(PCM 126/1964)

The tug *Assurance,* taking the half-submerged Holland No 2 submarine to Haslar Creek to place the vessel on the mud, for examination at low tide. The Holland-class coastal submarines were the first British submarines. Five were built by Vickers Barrow 1901-02. They spent their service lives defending Portsmouth and on training duty. They were all out of commission by 1913. No 2 was used in 1911 for target practice with grenades and primitive depth charges.

(PCRO 1083A)

Horses being ferried across the harbour *c*.1890. A horse ferry boat was first established between Portsmouth and Gosport in 1834.

(PCRO 418A/1/1)

A horsedrawn wagon disembarking from the Floating Bridge, *c*.1910. The Floating Bridge Company was incorporated in 1838 and commenced running in 1840.
(PCRO 49/8/1/3)

M.V.Shanklin at the harbour station in a watercolour by W. Jefferies, painted *c*.1960. The vessel was bought for the Portsmouth-Ryde service by British Railways in 1951. The harbour station was opened in 1876 to give a direct link between ferries and railway.
(PCM 474/1970)

Warships fire a salute as a steamer flying the royal ensign enters the harbour. She is probably HMS *Ophir*, bringing the Duke of York (later George V) back to England after a tour to Singapore, South Africa and Canada in 1901. An oil painting by E. Robins.   (PCM 476/1945)

Entrance to Portsmouth Harbour, an etching by W.L.Wyllie published in 1911. A spritsail barge and a larger sailing ship under tow from a tug are two of a variety of small vessels using the port. The narrow and easily-defended entrance to the harbour shown in this engraving was one of its attractions as a naval base.   (PCM 296/1948)

A small sailing ship leaves Portsmouth Harbour, *c.*1845. This watercolour by C.J.M.Whichelo demonstrates how close inshore the deep-water channel lies.
(PCM 51/1958)

HMS *Warrior*, at her berth on The Hard, 1992. In the background a visiting American warship enters harbour.
(PCRO Reprogr. 53/92/A10)

The Round Tower, constructed between 1418 and 1426, was one of a pair of towers built to protect a boom across the harbour mouth. The tower on the Gosport side was of wood. To the right of it is Eighteen-Gun Battery, first built by Sir Bernard de Gomme, a Dutch engineer, in the late 1680s. Both fortifications have been heavily modified. From a watercolour by W.E.Atkins.   (PCM 438/1959)

The boom across the harbour mouth *c.*1910, revived to protect against torpedo-boat attack. The Gosport chain ferry can be seen on the left, Quebec House centre-right.   (PCM)

The Square Tower was built by Henry VII in 1494. It served as the governor of the town's residence, and subsequently as a magazine and a victualling store. In 1821-22 a wooden tower was erected on top, supporting a post with semaphore arms which could transmit messages to Spithead or London. It was demolished in 1848. The landing stage outside the Sally Port became the Victoria Pier in 1842.   (PCM 1249/1987)

The first Quay Gate, from White Hart Road on to the Camber quay, *c.*1870. Note the workman in waistcoat and bowler hat, the gaslamp and carts.   (PCM 80/1965)

Also leading on to the Camber was King George's, or Quay, Gate, erected in 1734.   **(PCM 190/1977)**

King James' Gate, built in 1687, stood across Broad Street a short distance west of White Hart Road. The site of the moat on the Point side is now shown by the bridge which carries the promenade along the nearby ramparts.

(PCM 185/1977)

Landport Gate was the principal entry into Old Portsmouth from de Gomme's remodelling of the town in the 1660s until the ramparts were demolished. The structure dates from 1760, but its design is attributed to Nicholas Hawksmoor, it being put up after his death.

(PCM 181/1977)

King William Gate was cut through the ramparts of Old Portsmouth in 1834 to give access to Southsea along Pembroke Road.

(PCM 188/1977)

The Spur Redoubt stood in front of the Long Curtain, its guns intended to bombard attacking ships sailing up the channel to Portsmouth Harbour. It was one of Sir Bernard de Gomme's fortifications of the 1660s and 1670s. A ravelin was designed to provide no cover to any attacker who seized it. Access from it into the fortifications is along a narrow bridge across the moat.   (PCM 52/1952)

A view across Southsea Common towards the town, *c*.1800. The shutter telegraph can be seen dug into the glacis. Behind are the ramparts, with trees along them, the tower of St Thomas' church and, above the soldiers, the semaphore used to communicate with ships at Spithead. The wall on the left is Southsea Castle.   (PCM 419/1945)

A shutter telegraph station was built on the shore beside Old Portsmouth in 1796, one of a chain of stations to transmit messages rapidly between Spithead and the Admiralty in London. The naval lieutenant and men operating the shutters lived in the building beneath them. The service was discontinued in 1816. (PCM 735/1945)

Lion Gate, across Queen Street, photographed from the inside *c.*1870. The stonework of the gate has been incorporated in the Dockyard's Semaphore Tower. (PCM 849/1980)

Unicorn Gate, 1778, photographed *c.*1870. It originally stood at the northern end of York Place, beside Anglesea Barracks. Resited, it is now an entrance to the Naval barracks.   (PCM 186/1977)

Southsea Castle was built by Henry VIII in 1544-5. It was one of a string of forts along the south coast to counter possible French invasion. This watercolour shows it in the mid eighteenth century, before the modifications of 1814.

(PCM 1p/1987/28)

Fort Cumberland, built to prevent French invasion boats entering Langstone Harbour, is the best-preserved star fort in Britain. Between 1747 and 1750 earthen ramparts were thrown up. In 1782 the Duke of Richmond ordered its reconstruction on a larger scale and in stone and brick. It was completed in 1810. Much of the work was done by convicts.   (PCM)

Ramparts and moat at Hilsea, part of the Hilsea Lines constructed 1861-2, *c.*1950. The height of the ramparts from the bed of the moat was approximately 40 feet. Together with the swing bridge constructed over the channel separating Portsea Island from the mainland they formed a formidable defence. Obsolete soon after they were completed, the Lines were breached in due course to improve entrance to and egress from the town.   (PCRO DL/P)

Hilsea Lagoon, nd. Originally part of the defensive moat constructed in 1861-2. This photograph illustrates admirably the road layout before the Hilsea roundabout was constructed and, subsequently, the M27.   (PCRO 1518A/1/70)

On the left is the Nelson memorial, on the right Fort Nelson under construction. The fort was built to prevent French forces landing east of Portsmouth and attacking the island from inland. Before the fort was completed the French had become allies, and this engraving was published in 1865 when their fleet visited as part of an Anglo-French sabre rattling aimed at the Yankees.   (PCM 29/1962)

Fort Widley was one of a chain of forts constructed between 1862 and 1867 along the crest of Portsdown Hill. Many people doubted that these forts were necessary and they were dubbed 'Palmerston's Follies' after the Prime Minister of the day. The government, however, feared that enemies attacking Portsmouth from the north could bombard the Dockyard with the newly-developed, long-range rifled cannon: the forts guarded against this danger. Behind the fort can be seen the short-lived Portsdown Park development.

(PCM 21/1979

Spitbank Fort, one of the four forts in the Solent that Lord Palmerston also ordered built, in 1863, to protect Spithead and the Dockyard from seaborne attack by the new armoured warships. Construction proved difficult and they were not finished until 1880.

(PCM)

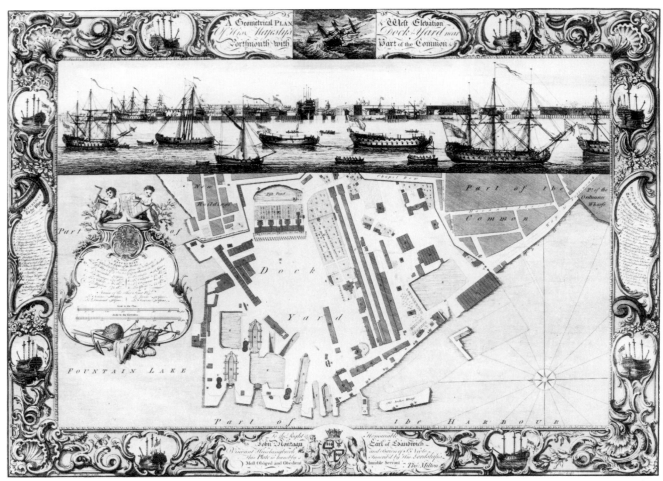

A panorama of the Dockyard in 1754.   (PCM)

The launch of an unidentified vessel, perhaps the *Neptune*, in 1832. This 120-gun battleship would have had many iron parts, allowing it to be built much larger than the *Victory*. Launches were always popular public occasions.   (PCM)

The launch of the steam frigate *Dauntless* on 5 January 1847. She was the second propeller-driven vessel to be built in the Dockyard. Behind her are the sheds sheltering the building slips. (PCM 252/1964)

The Dockyard was often used by troopships. On 12 May 1856 a transport carrying hussars, lancers and invalids returning from the Crimea docked there. Queen Victoria was in Portsmouth and an impromptu review was held. A watercolour by R.H.Ubsdell. (PCM 187/1945)

The Naval Academy was built in 1729-32, the octagonal tower and dome were added in 1808. The academy provided an academic training for boys entering the Navy as officers, but most learnt the job at sea. It was reconstituted as the Royal Naval College in 1808.   (PCM 941/1974)

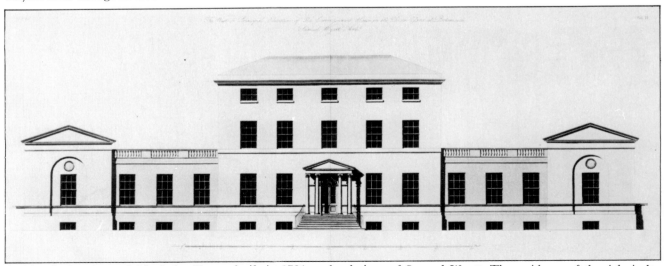

Architect's drawings of Admiralty House, built in 1784 to the designs of Samuel Wyatt. The residence of the Admiralty Commissioner for the Dockyard, in the nineeenth century it became the home of the Commander-in-Chief, Portsmouth. The original porch has been replaced and a cupola added, but otherwise the building is much as constructed.

(PCM 232/1945)

Admiralty House, *c*.1910.   (PCRO 151A/7/61)

Long Row, Portsmouth Dockyard. Built 1717, with alterations in the early nineteenth century, for senior Naval officers of the Dockyard establishment. The southernmost house with its large garden became the official residence of the Admiral Superintendent of the Dockyard in 1832. Most of Long Row is now office accommodation.   (PCRO 187A/8)

FITTING BASIN, LOOKING NORTH

DEEP DOCK

THE ROPE WALK

THE SEMAPHORE AND ARCHWAY LEADING TO TROOPERS JETTY

STEM OF THE "COLLINGWOOD" DOCKED

MAST HOUSE, TORPEDO BOATS, AND PRINCE OF WALES'S FISHING BOAT

NASMYTH'S HAMMER

"Colossus"   "Cyclops"   "Rupert" FITTING BASIN

MOULD LOFT

DOCK GATES, LOOKING OUT

This group of illustrations from *The Graphic* in 1885 demonstrates the variety of work carried out in the Dockyard. Government and repair, but it built many vessels including the first of each of the Dreadnought classes.

THE OLD BASIN

TORPEDO LAUNCHES IN OBSOLETE DOCK

THE "MEDINA," A LARGE MODERN GUNBOAT IN OLD DOCK

CHAIN-TESTING ROOM

Exterior of Rope Walk

"Devastation" "Active"

KING'S ROAD

ANCHOR LANE

policy was to make the yard as independent of outside contractors as possible. Portsmouth's main role was fitting out

Employment in the Dockyard was not always secure in the nineteenth century although far more men worked there in 1900 than in 1800. There were mass lay-offs in 1816, 1857, 1868-9 and 1887. This engraving shows redundant dockyardmen boarding a troopship provided by the government to help them emigrate to Canada in 1869.　　　　　(PCM)

London Road, Portsdown, by George Cole, 1867, painted from near the *George.* This picture demonstrates how rural Portsea Island was during the nineteenth century — and how bad Britain's roads were. It is no wonder that the development of railways provided such a fillip to the economy. In the foreground is one of Portsdown's chalkpits, providing raw material for a lime kiln.
(PCM 3/1954)

Cosham and Portsea Island, 1908, watercolour. The northern parts of Portsea Island and the mainland around Cosham remained pretty rural until after 1918. A Portsdown and Horndean Light Railway tram creeps up the hill in the foreground — the embankment for the line can still be traced.
(PCM 43/1958)

Portsmouth Harbour, *c.*1938. This watercolour shows the broad expanse of sheltered water that made the harbour such a valuable anchorage. An admiralty report of 1774 said there were moorings for 62 ships. The Roman and medieval fort at Portchester, in the middleground, demonstrates the long history of the harbour as a naval base.　　　(PCM 373/1945)

North End, 1870. The area was then a suburban hamlet on the road to London, but it was shortly to become a tramway terminus.

(PCM)

The Connaught Drill Hall, Stanhope Road, was one of the victims of the heavy raid of 10 January 1941. There were 171 people killed in this, the most damaging raid of the war, 430 injured and the homes of some 3,000 destroyed. The Guildhall and Commercial Road, Kings Road and Palmerston Road shopping centres were also burnt down.
(PCM 446/1945)

A theatre was built on the east side of the High Street in 1761 and demolished to make way for the Cambridge Barracks in 1854. This watercolour shows it between 1821 and the remodelling of its façade in 1831. Note the gas lamp and lamplighter with his ladder.
(PCM 106/1943)

Portsmouth High Street looking south-west, c.1830. The market house, with the council chamber over it, was built in 1739 and demolished in 1836. The elegant Georgian houses which predominate on the street were the result of the town's prosperity during the eighteenth century, achieved through preparing the fleet for war with France.
(PCM 103/1964)

A painting by Richrd Ubsdell of the Town Hall in the High Street. It shows the building as it was between 1795, when a portico at the south-western end was replaced by an extension supported on Ionic columns, and 1827, when the butchers' shambles were cleared away. The picture was probably painted some years later. A procession of civic dignitaries, the aldermen in their red gowns and councillors in black gowns, is ascending to the council chamber.
(PCM 863/1946)

The Saluting Platform, first built *c.*1500, was a popular spot for a promenade. The building with the cupola was the Signal House, built 1569, on the right is the Courts-martial House, erected 1682. The sundial was placed there in 1718; it is now in the Lumps Fort rose garden. The clothes of the figures suggest that this painting dates from *c.*1730.
(PCM 74/1953)

Sailors, their wives, families, sweethearts and prostitutes carouse or bid each other farewell on Portsmouth Point. Death at sea through disease, accident or battle was common, while voyages could last for years. Sailors would receive their pay and prize money (a share of the value of captured vessels) in lump sums when they reached port. Their lives were so uncertain that many spent it as soon as they could. Thomas Rowlandson made the sketch for this engraving in 1800.
(PCM 605/1945)

On the Point, Portsmouth, 1857, by William Smyth. Centre-right are the terminal buildings for the chain ferry to Gosport. Around it are many wherries, as small ferryboats were known in the district. The ferry destroyed the wherrymen's trade to Gosport, but they still had plenty of business taking passengers to ships in the harbour. Behind is the *Quebec Hotel*.
(PCM 68/1982)

In the foreground is the Camber dry dock, built 1860, and under construction behind is Portsmouth's first power station, opened in 1894. The building on the left is a board school. This watercolour is by Martin Snape. **(PCM 191/1945)**

The Camber, Portsmouth,
watercolour by Maurice Clarke.
This picture shows the lively
character of the Camber not long
after 1945. The buildings on the
far right are Vospers boatyard.
(PCM 141/1975)

Entrance to Portsmouth Harbour,
watercolour by Clarkson Stanfield,
1829. Centre-right is the Square
Tower, surmounted by the
wooden tower erected in 1822 to
support a semaphore and
accommodate its operators. On the
right are the tower of St Thomas'
Church and Burridge's Folly,
which stood on the Baltic Wharf
beside the Camber.
(PCM 256/1982)

The harbour defences, painted
from Fort Blockhouse in 1881 by
H.Coish, a local artist. The sweep
of Portsmouth's seafront defences
from the Round Tower to the
King's Bastion is clearly depicted
save the Square Tower, which is
hidden by the nearer sailing boat.
(PCM 125/1964)

The royal yacht steams through a crowded harbour. Behind it is the original Semaphore Tower in the Dockyard, which burnt down in 1913. The nearer of the wooden warships is the *Victory*, behind her is HMS *Wellington*. Both have their upper decks roofed over to increase the accommodation they offered. (PCM 80/1959)

Old Hulks, by W.L.Wyllie, 1880. Many warships superceded by developments in naval technology continued to serve as training ships, barracks, explosive stores and for a variety of other purposes. Shore establishments replaced them only early in the twentieth century.
(PCM 294/1964)

HMS *Victory* was moored in Portsmouth Harbour throughout the nineteenth century. In 1922 she was berthed in the oldest drydock in the Dockyard and restored to the condition she was at Trafalgar. W.L.Wyllie was a leading proponent of her restoration. He painted this watercolour of her and HMS *Royal Sovereign* for a publicity poster in 1928.
(PCM 378/1945)

Bathing machines on Southsea Beach, *c.*1800. They were first recorded here, where the King's Rooms later stood, now the site of the funfair, in the 1770s. The hoods allowed the bathers to enter the water in privacy. Bathing machines remained in use until World War One.   (PCM 79/1962)

Left: *The interior of the Garrison Church*, 1873, gouache by Col.R.C.Goff. The Church was built in the twelfth century as the chapel of the Domus Dei hospital and almshouse. After the Reformation it became the chapel for the governor's house. It was drastically restored in 1868, but the nave was destroyed by German bombs.   (PCM 84/1959)
Right: The Worcestershire Regiment (of militia) being reviewed on Southsea Common in 1800. Militia regiments were usually used to garrison Portsmouth during the Napoleonic Wars. An oil painting by Richard Livesay.   (PCM 112/1960)

The construction of the new entrance to No.2 Basin (the Steam Basin built in 1843-8), during the Great Extension. This work was completed in 1873 using steam-powered cranes.   (PCM 105/1980)

A vessel in No.12 Dock when newly opened in 1876. This dock was one of the first of those constructed during the 'Great Extension' of the Dockyard which took place during the 1870s. The new docks covered some 158 acres of mostly reclaimed mudland and more than doubled the size of the Dockyard. They were necessary to cope with the growing size of the new iron-built, steam-powered warships.   (PCM 558/1978)

Main Gate, c.1910. The Main Gate has piers of Portland stone. The Pier on the eastern side is in its original position; the pier on the western side was set back in 1942 to widen the gate. The dockyard wall was built 1704-11, probably replacing a simple palisade, bank and ditch. With the Porters Lodge, now stuccoed, built 1708, these were the first brick structures in the dockyard.   (PCRO 187A/6)

The Steam Hammer, c.1910. The steam hammer stood in the smithery, a tubular, metal-frame building hung with corrugated-iron sheeting and completed in 1852. It had more the atmosphere of premises in the Black Country than a south coast town.
(PCRO 694A/9/1/144)

A mast under construction in the Dockyard in the 1930s. There are also piles of blocks on the nearby work bench.
(PCRO 496A/1/63)

The interior of Middle Building, Wood Mills, nd, showing some of Brunel's pulley block making machinery. Between 1802 and 1806, 45 machines for the manufacture of pulley blocks, designed by Marc Brunel and built by Henry Maudslay, were installed in Portsmouth Dockyard. These were the first metal machines installed anywhere in the world for mass, but not flow, production. Ten men now did the work of 110 craftsmen manufacturing 140,000 pulley blocks per annum.
(PCRO 694A/9/1/145)

HMS *Calliope* in dry dock, nd. A screw corvette, she was built in Portsmouth Dockyard in 1884. She became a RNVR drill ship in 1907. She was renamed the *Helicon* in 1915 but reverted to *Calliope* in 1931. She was broken up in 1951.

The Dockyard fire station, nd. This building was constructed *c*.1843. The iron structure of two tiers of arched girders above circular columns tied with bracing enclosed a 770 tons capacity metal water tank which not only supplied a ring main serving the major buildings in the dockyard but also supplied cooling water for steam engines' condensers. The tank has now been removed. The framework, clad with corrugated iron, served for many years as the Dockyard fire station.

(PCRO 187A/7)

A torpedo boat destroyer in No 4 Dock, *c*.1910, one of the four stone-built docks opening off the Great Ship Basin reconstructed 1795-1801 by Brigadier-General Sir Samuel Bentham, brother of Jeremy Bentham, who had become Inspector General of Naval Works in 1795.

(PCRO 187A/1/1)

HMS *Prince George* in dry dock, probably one of Bentham's docks, nd.   (PCRO 187A/12)

The launch of the *Iron Duke*, 12 October 1912, the most powerful yet of the Dreadnoughts. The *Iron Duke* was launched in the presence of a crowd of 60,000 by the Duchess of Wellington.
(PCRO 681A/1/9/20)

Two contrasting warships. One of the new submarines passes HMS *Dreadnought* and a paddle steamer moored by the Dockyard Camber, *c*.1910.
(PCM 653/1945p)

The old Semaphore Station, destroyed by fire in 1913.

(PCRO 187A/9)

Acetylene welding of ventilation trunks in No.1 Shipbuilding Shop, 1917. Women workers came into the Dockyard in large numbers for the first time during World War One, doing tasks which had previously been male preserves. Most were discharged in peacetime. (PCM)

A coastal vessel moored near the Round Tower in 1948, painted by D.Rose. The Round Tower was built in 1683 on the shore beside the Dockyard. It was re-erected on the outer quay of the Great Extension in the 1870s. Behind is the 250-ton hammer-head crane, the largest in the world when it was constructed in 1912. (PCM 1110/1980a)

The Naval Ordnance Depot, HM Gunwharf, latterly HMS *Vernon*. The foundation stone of this magnificent storehouse was laid 28 November 1811 by HRH the Duke of Clarence. In 1827 local historian Dr Slight wrote: 'It contains the battering-train, gun-carriages, and every description of ordnance store ready at a moment's notice!'   (PCRO 1132A/1/2/6)

A view from the power station chimney, *c.*1905. In the left foreground are the buildings of the Gunwharf, now HMS *Vernon*. Just beyond it two paddle steamers are moored in front of the harbour station, and the Semaphore Tower in the Dockyard occupies the centre of the picture.
(PCM 755/1964)

A young Japanese officer shows an English lady around his warship on a visit to the Dockyard in 1911. Japan had a powerful and modern navy, which in 1905 had heavily defeated the Imperial Russian Navy at the Battle of Tsushima.

(PCM 649/1945o)

Navy Days, late 1920s. Crowds queue to board HMS *Victory*. *Victory* was towed to her last berth in the oldest dock in Portsmouth Dockyard on 12 January 1922 to save her from complete collapse.   (PCRO DL/P)

Naval and Garrison Town

George III reviewing the fleet at Spithead, probably in 1773 or 1778. A watercolour by the king's Marine Painter, Dominic Serres RA (1722-93), of one of the first naval reviews at Portsmouth.   (PCM 724/1979)

During the middle years of the nineteenth century a series of immensely popular naval reviews were held at Spithead. Here sightseers are disembarking from small boats after trips around the 1856 review at which there were 254 Royal Navy vessels.
(PCM 12/1960)

The Baltic Fleet leaving Spithead, 1855. At the outbreak of the Crimean War a fleet was fitted out at Portsmouth to fight the Russians in the north. It achieved nothing of significance.
(PCM)

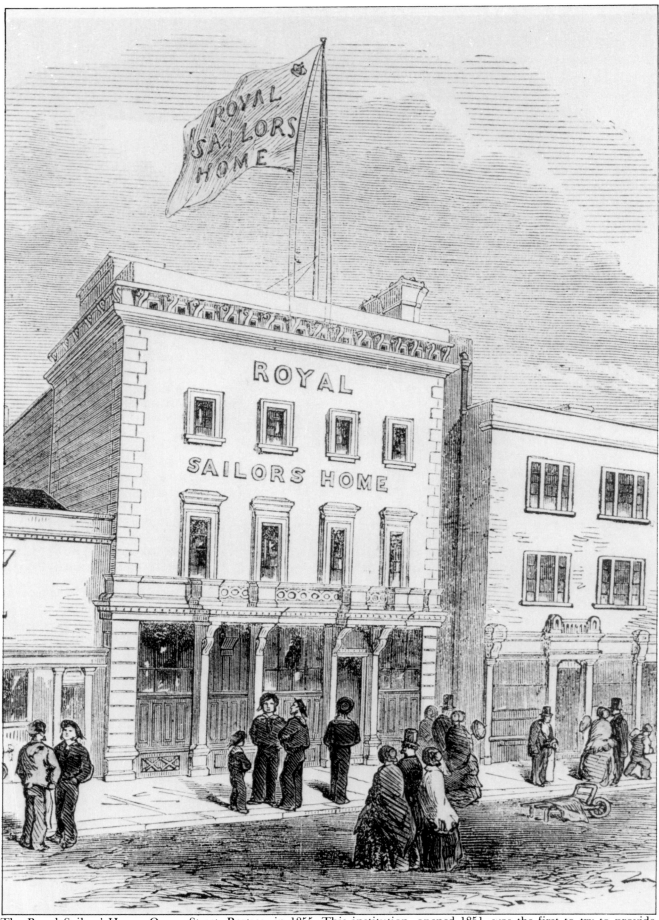

The Royal Sailors' Home, Queen Street, Portsea, in 1855. This institution, opened 1851, was the first to try to provide some alternative to the pub for the sailor on shore leave.

(PCM 18P/1988)

The Sailors' Rest, in Landport, was set up in 1881 to provide refreshments, recreation and accommodation for sailors on leave. Its founder Agnes Weston, depicted in the roundel, was created a dame for her work in looking after the physical and moral welfare of Britain's sailors.
(PCM 23p/1988)

The dining hall of the Trafalgar Institute.
(PCRO 884A/1/4/5)

The Trafalgar Institute — the Church of England Soldiers' and Sailors' Institute — provided shore accommodation for servicemen. Its progress was impressive. It opened on 14 December 1906 in premises in Edinburgh Road occupied originally by the YMCA and afterwards the *Southern Daily Mail*. It was further extended in 1907, 1912 and 1926. (PCRO 884A/1/4/7)

Prior to 1845, Whale Island was covered at every Spring tide but the dumping of mud excavated for the new steam basin in the dockyard succeeded in raising the island ten to fifteen feet above sea level. In 1861 the Government purchased Whale Island from the Corporation.

A gunnery school was first established in 1830 on Collingwood's old ship HMS *Excellent* moored then in Portsmouth Harbour. Such was the success of the venture that in due course more spacious accommodation was required and Whale Island, which had been used for some time by HMS *Excellent* as a rifle range, was selected for the purpose. The school was finally transferred ashore in 1891.

(PCRO 187A/4)

The main gate of the naval barracks. These barracks were the scene of a mutiny and rioting by stokers in 1906. The trigger was the order 'On the knee' given by a gunnery officer to the stokers on parade. It was interpreted by them as an attempt to humiliate them.

(PCM 1077/1980b)

(PCM 246/1946)

The officers' mess of the Royal Naval Barracks. This large barrack complex was erected in 1899-1903 on land formerly part of the defences of Portsea. Until then sailors in Portsmouth had to sleep on hulks moored in the harbour.

The Royal Marine Artillery Barracks in the Gunwharf, in 1855. These barracks were occupied from 1824 until 1858, when the unit moved to Fort Cumberland. (PCM 13/1983/6)

A battalion of the Royal Marine Artillery prepare to march to Southsea Common for an inspection, 1868. The Eastney Barracks were completed in 1860 and the Marine Artillery moved into them from Fort Cumberland. (PCRO 1403A/2/1)

The guard parade outside the guardhouse on Grand Parade, *c.*1870.   (PCM 933/1974)

Troops being inspected on Governor's Green, *c.*1871. In the background is the Headquarters of the 1st
Hants Artillery Volunteers.   (PCRO 1403A/2/2/)

Royal Marine Artillery leaving Portsmouth to embark at Plymouth 'for the front'. Judging from the uniforms this was probably during the Boer War. The picture was taken for use in a stereoscopic viewer. (PCM 1103/1980)

Troop inspection on Southsea Common, *c.*1880. The view of the houses in the background has changed very little in the last one hundred years.   (PCRO 1079A/1/4)

Military manoeuvres on Southsea Common, *c.*1875.   (PCRO 738A/5)

A large-scale military exercise involving a mock battle was held in Portsmouth in 1867. Many of the soldiers involved were part-timers. Here the 'defending force' concentrates at King William's Gate. (PCM 39p/1988)

Old Government House in the High Street before 1882. In that year it was vacated for the new Government House built on land formerly part of the glacis of the old fortifications opposite Landport Terrace. Old Government House was formerly the residence of the Naval Commander-in-Chief and many famous men and women were received on its premises.

(PCRO 1079A/1/8)

New Government House, completed 1882. (PCRO 1079A/1/1)

Troops marching along Penny Street, *c.*1920. (PCRO 1076A/2)

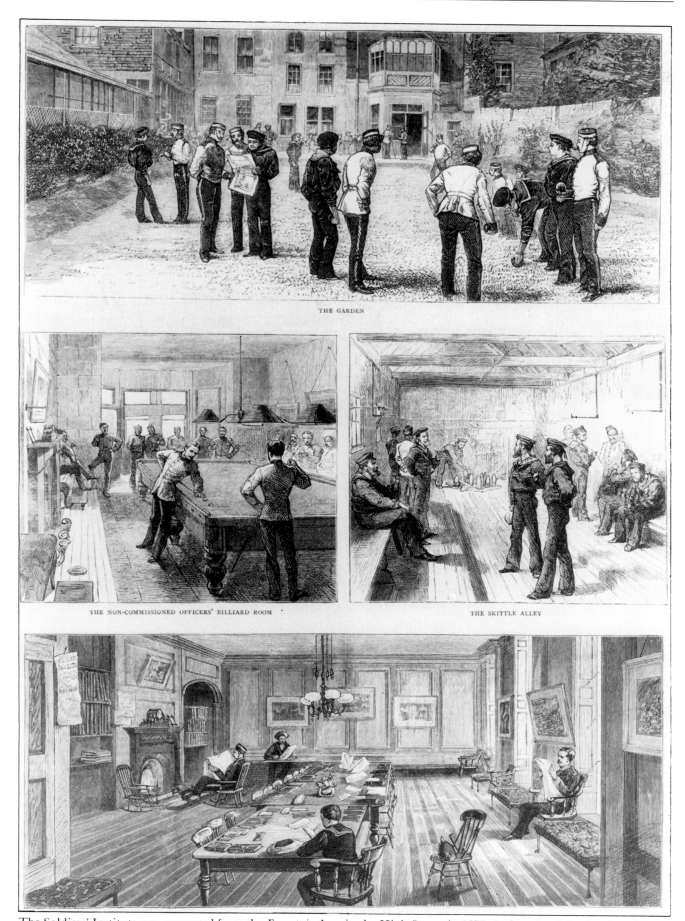

THE GARDEN

THE NON-COMMISSIONED OFFICERS' BILLIARD ROOM · THE SKITTLE ALLEY

The Soldiers' Institute was converted from the *Fountain Inn*, in the High Street, in 1875. Its founder, Miss Sarah Robinson, was burnt in effigy on Southsea Common by its opponents, mostly 'land sharks and women'. It provided for the soldiers of the garrison similar facilities to the Sailors' Rest.

(PCM 24p/1988)

The Royal Garrison Church: Church Parade, 1896-7. The building is all that remains of the ancient hospice, Domus Dei founded *c*.1212, which occupied parts of what is now Governor's Green as well as land lying to the south of the church toward the sea. It was surrendered in 1540 and in due course became the Governor's residence. The marriage

of Charles II with Catherine of Braganza was celebrated in the Governor's house on 21 May 1662. It ceased to be the Governor's residence by the beginning of the nineteenth century although the allied sovereigns met here in a series of glittering ceremonies in June 1814. Save for the chapel, the complex was demolished in 1826. (PCRO 194A/3/21)

Troops marching past the Guildhall steps, nd.   (PCRO 18A/2/1)

March Past at the Victoria Barracks, *c.*1900. In the 1880s the great barrack complex to the east of the High Street was further extended over the site of the recently-demolished fortifications. Clarence Barracks were greatly enlarged and a new complex, the Victoria Barracks, built. Only one block survives of Victoria Barracks, the present City Museum. The adjoining NAAFI premises are now the City Records Office. The rest of the site was demolished *c.*1970.   (PCRO 1488A/1/1)

A watercolour, by James Calcott, of the Town Hall from the south *c.*1826. This building was erected in 1738-9 and demolished in 1836. Its ground floor served as a market house, but it was necessary also to have stalls in the street. By this date permanent shops with big display windows such as those in this picture sold more valuable items.

(PCM 132/1952)

Opening of the Town Hall by TRH The Prince and Princess of Wales, 9 August 1890. Work had begun in August 1886 when the mayor, Mr Alfred S. Blake, laid the foundation stone.

(PCRO 1499A/34)

The foundation stone of a fine new Town Hall in the Doric style was laid on 24 May 1837. The architect was Benjamin Bramble, later several times mayor. The ground floor was used as a market hall. It became a museum in 1895.   (PCM)

The Town Hall *en fête* for the visit of the French Northern Squadron, August 1905. King Edward VII reviewed the Fleet on 9 August. Officers and men were entertained ashore and according to a contemporary observer 'the scenes in the streets where our sailors fraternized joyously with the visitors will never be forgotten . . .'. (PCRO 1607A/1)

Ceremony to mark the extension of the Portsmouth borough boundary to Hilsea. For the first time, the borough boundary now encompassed the whole of Portsea Island.   (PCRO 11A/27/146)

Mayor's Sunday at St Thomas' Church. The mayor, Alderman Corbin, and Party including the Town Clerk, Mr Frederick Sparks, and the mace bearer, 1924.   (PCRO 998A/1/4)

The Rt.Hon. David Lloyd George, OM, MP, is presented with the Freedom of the Borough by the Mayor, Alderman Corbin, 27 September 1924.

(PCRO 998A/1/40)

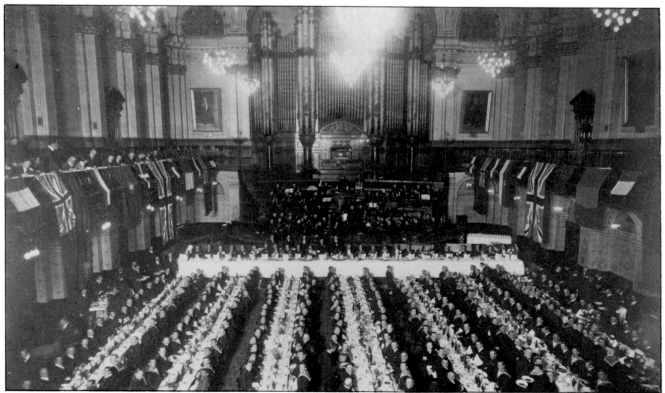

Lower Deck Dinner, Town Hall, nd.

(PCRO 45A/11/1)

Portsmouth Guildhall, 1988. The Guildhall was burnt out on the night of 10-11 January 1941. It was rebuilt within the 1890 shell to new designs by E. Berry Webber 1955-8 and re-opened by HM the Queen, 8 June 1959.

(PCRO Reprogr. 99/88/A1)

The Mayor and Mayoress, Alderman and Mrs Corbin, pose with their family party at the Mayor and Mayoress' Childrens' Fancy Dress Ball, 9 January 1924.   (PCRO 998A/1/20)

The Assembled Company at the Childrens' Fancy Dress Ball, 9 January 1924.   (PCRO 998A/1/24)

Choirs singing on the Town Hall steps, Easter Sunday 1909.   (PCRO 342A/2/4)

The opening of Portsmouth Municipal College, 10 September 1908. The ceremony was performed by Councillor F.G.Foster, a widower, who installed his small daughter, Doris, aged 5½, as mayoress. Doris can be seen on the steps with her father.
(PCRO 681A/3/3/7)

The Portsmouth Borough Police Force, *c.*1860. The force was established in 1836 by the newly-reformed Borough Council as one of their first acts following the municipal elections on 26 December 1835. (PCRO 1201A/2)

Members of Portsmouth's fire brigade sit proudly on their steam-powered fire-engine outside the city's Technical Institute and library, built in 1908. The photograph was taken in 1912. At this date the town's firemen were members of the police force. (PCM 15/1980)

Portsmouth Borough Fire Brigade engines outside the Technical Institute in 1921. (PCM 118/1975)

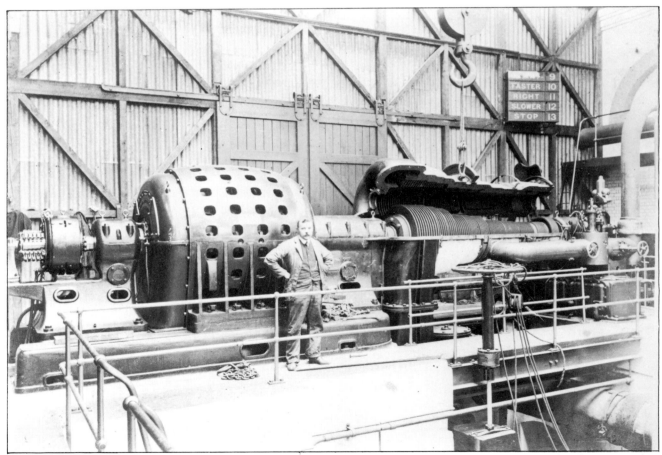

The borough council decided to supply the town with electricity. It built a generating station near the Camber, convenient for colliers, which opened in 1894. Here a workman poses before a 1,000kw turbo-alternator. (PCM 757/1964)

Once the new Town Hall in Commercial Road had opened in 1890 the old Town Hall in the High Street was redundant. In 1895 it was opened as a museum and by 1901 it had over 45,000 visitors a year. The building and almost all its contents were destroyed by German bombing in 1941. (PCM 1056/1980)

Easter Monday Parade of dustmen with their horses (decorated with flowers and bells) outside the old Council Depot in Spring Gardens. The winning horses display their certificates. (PCRO 434A/2)

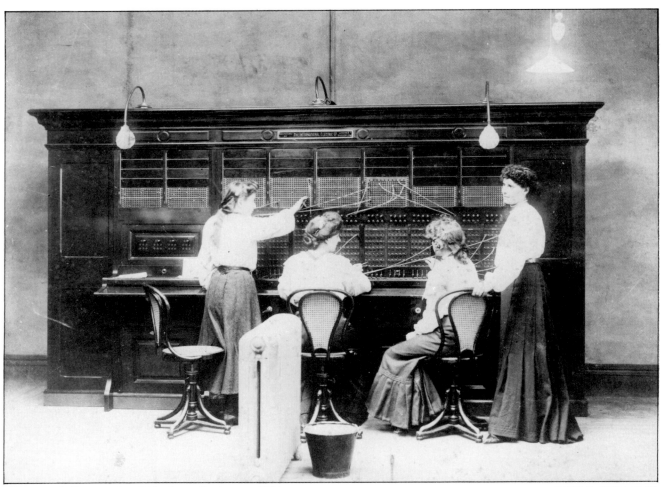

Portsmouth Corporation Telephone Exchange, 1904. (PCRO 1008A/1/1)

The first lady magistrates are added to the Commission of the Peace for Portsmouth, April 1924: Mrs Jane Kingswell, Mrs E.J.Long and Miss B.W.Reading. (PCRO 998A/1/26)

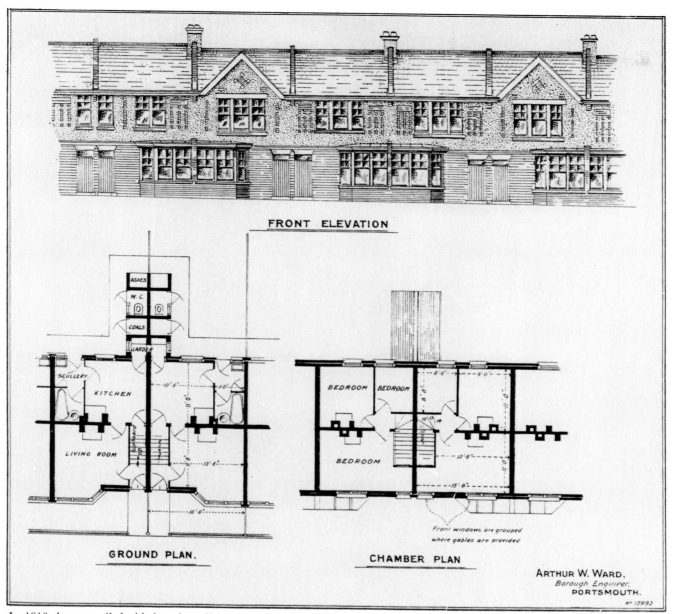

FRONT ELEVATION

GROUND PLAN.

CHAMBER PLAN

ARTHUR W. WARD,
Borough Engineer,
PORTSMOUTH.

In 1910 the council decided to demolish an area of slum housing in Portsea and build a new street, Curzon Howe Road, containing 46 houses. These, Portsmouth's first council houses, provided high quality accommodation. Upstairs were three bedrooms, one for the parents and one for the children of each sex. Downstairs was a large front room, a back kitchen, a scullery and, partitioned off from it, a bath. Hot water was provided from a copper built in beside the bath. A single-storey extension at the back housed the outside lavatory. *(PCRO MOH report, 1913)*

Portsmouth's councillors knew that the city would be desperately short of houses when World War Two ended. In 1944 they bought land near Havant on which to build when the war ended and in September 1947 construction of the Leigh Park estate began. This is Prospect Farm, recently completed in 1965. *(PCM 622/1977)*

HM the Queen watches the band of the Royal Marines in Guildhall Square on the occasion of the Australian Bicentennial celebrations, 13 May 1987. The First Fleet set sail from Portsmouth with more than 1,500 people on board on 13 May 1787. Convicts, soldiers, sailors and children, they were the founders of modern Australia.   (PCRO Reprogr. 88/87/812)

Lord Charles Beresford (right) campaigning in Portsmouth during one or other of the General Election campaigns of 1910.
(PCRO 1083A/1/2/64)

Places of Worship

'Kingston Church Hants' by R.H.C.Ubsdell, 1842. This is a watercolour of the old medieval St Mary's Portsea. Endowed *c*.1164, it was the first church built on Portsea Island.
(PCM 721/45)

In 1843 a new St Mary's was built, to accommodate the growing local population, by Southsea architect Thomas Ellis Owen. The new church was built of flint with stone quoins. Curiously, the old tower of the medieval church was retained, dwarfed by the tall nave of the new church.   (PCM 91/60)

Exterior and interior of the present St Mary's Portsea built 1887-9 to designs of Sir Arthur Blomfield, to replace the 1843 church which in its turn no longer provided adequate seating for an ever-increasing congregation.

(PCRO 694A/9/1/97-8)

Mid-nineteenth-century view of the interior of St Thomas' Church, Portsmouth. Built *c.*1180 by Norman merchant, Jean de Gisors, St Thomas' was badly damaged during the Civil War by Parliamentary guns. The tower and nave were rebuilt — the nave in the classical style of the day — in the late seventeenth century. Restoration work by local architect Thomas Ellis Owen in the early nineteenth century put in place the steeply pointed chancel arch. (PCM)

A recent view of Old Portsmouth and the Cathedral Church of St Thomas of Canterbury. St Thomas's was chosen to be the cathedral church of the new Anglican diocese of Portsmouth when it was created out of the ancient diocese of Winchester in 1927. Partially extended in 1938-9 by Sir Charles Nicholson, it was only completed in 1991 to new designs by Michael Drury. (PCC Reprogr. 150/92/M10)

St John's Chapel, Portsea, 1861. Built 1787-8, St John's stood in Prince George Street, Portsea. It was a proprietary chapel of evangelical persuasion where pews could be both bought and sold.

(PCM 70/1983B)

St George's Church, Portsea, *c.*1910. This was the first church to be built to cope with the growing local population in the early eighteenth century. The foundation stone was laid in 1753. A proprietary chapel, St George's was a chapel of ease to the mother church of St Mary's Portsea.

(PCM 1015/1980)

St Paul's Chapel, Southsea. St Paul's Chapel was built with funds from a parliamentary commission formed to help build new churches in the industrial towns. It was designed by Francis Goodwin and built 1820-2. It was burnt out in 1941 during air raids although the walls and cast-iron tracery were not actually demolished until 1959.

(PCM)

Interior of the Synagogue in The Thicket, Southsea. The early history of the Jewish synagogues in Portsmouth is sketchy.
The first was probably in Oyster Street *c.*1716. The congregation probably moved to Daniel Street and then White's
Row in Portsea in the early eighteenth century. The move to The Thicket took place in 1936.

(PCM)

King Street Chapel in Portsea was built 1812-13 to provide increased accommodation for worshippers at the Congregational Orange Street Chapel. The new Chapel could seat some 2,500 people and soon became a great and thriving success under its popular pastor Mr John Griffin. It was numerically one of the largest chapels in the South of England.

(PCM 7P/1987)

Farlington Church. The earliest reference to a church at Farlington seems to be in 1200. The church was almost entirely rebuilt in 1872-5 by G.E.Street. Street was also employed in the restoration at Wymering, 1858-61.

(PCRO 549A/6/1/18)

The Roman Catholic Cathedral of St John the Evangelist in Edinburgh Road was built 1877-82 to designs by J.Crawley. Further additions were made in 1886 and 1892 by J.S.Hanson.   (PCRO 1518A/1/20)

St Swithun's Roman Catholic Church and the adjoining Presbytery in Waverley Road, Southsea. The parish church began life as a chapel of ease to the Roman Catholic Cathedral. The foundation stone for a new church to replace the old iron building was laid in 1895 but chronic shortages of funds meant that the task of completing the building was not actually finished until 1900-01.

(PCRO 460A/3/2)

The Circus Church, Landport was so-called because on 7 June 1857 there was first held an Evangelical service in a wooden building in Lion Gate Road known as The Circus. The service took place under the auspices of the Revd John Knapp of St John's Portsea. The experiment was a tremendous success from the beginning with crowds of over 2,000 people attending. In due course in 1864 permanent premises were built in Surrey Street and they were eventually licensed, but the Circus Church maintained always a rugged independence. The building was destroyed in 1941 during an air raid.

(PCM 1408/1974)

St Luke's Church has been described as a bastion of conservative Evangelicalism in the late nineteenth and early twentieth centuries. Established in the 1860s, St Luke's had a formidable reputation for out-reach work in its predominantly working-class district. There was a soup kitchen, a visiting society, a tract association, societies for young men and women, branches of the Band of Hope and Scripture Union, an industrial society and a mothers' meeting. The mission hall was in Marylebone Street.

(PCM)

Powerscourt Road Chapel in Powerscourt Road was Bible Christian. Established in 1900, it became a United Methodist Church in 1907. Redundant as a church in 1949 it was purchased for use as a church by the Lake Road Baptists, who had lost their premises in an air raid on 24 August 1940.   (PCRO 151A/7/80)

Buckland Congregational Church opened on 24 June 1869. A Sunday School had opened in a room in the area as early as 1810-11 under the leadership of staff from Orange Street. It was licensed shortly afterwards for worship and prospered. A purpose-built chapel was built and opened for worship in 1822. Increasing numbers and a general lack of space necessitated the building of the new church.
(PCRO 151A/7/81)

High Grove Farm, Baffins, early this century. Portsea Island was almost entirely agricultural land until the late nineteenth century, and many of its inhabitants were farmworkers. Their work was dominated by the daily rhythms of looking after animals and the annual rhythm of the seasons.

(PCM 467/1974)

After the Catch, fishing boats in the Camber, 1936.

(PCM 638/1945)

Tidying Up. The Camber in 1936. Portsmouth still has a fishing fleet, although it has never had a large one.

(PCM 671/1945)

Men and boys in J.D.Feltham's boat-building yard, *c.*1883. The yacht in the background is the *Bird of Freedom*.

(PCRO 1270A/10)

Shop of W.R.Wade, Gas Fitter and Paper Hanger, 106-8 Kingston Road, *c.*1880.

(PCRO 533A/1/1)

Unloading timber at Flathouse, 1936. Flathouse Wharf was given to the corporation in 1864 in compensation for Anchor Gate Wharf, which was taken into the Dockyard.   (PCM 674/1945)

Exterior and interior views of Treadgolds, Iron Merchants of Bishop Street, Portsea, *c*.1870. Treadgolds ceased trading only in 1988. Their premises, preserved quite remarkably, belong now to Hampshire County Council.

(PCRO 1057A/1/121/1&3)

The yard of Messrs Pike Spicer and Co Ltd, brewers, and a group photograph of their employees, 1911. The brewery was situated in Penny Street. The founder of the firm, William Pike, was born in Dorset in 1691. His father died when he was a child and in 1705 he was sent to Portsmouth to be apprenticed to his mother's cousin, William Mudge, who had begun business as a cooper in the mid-seventeenth century but who was by this time a considerable brewer. The young Pike inherited a sizeable share of his uncle's estate in 1719 and set up in business as a brewer himself shortly afterwards. He went into partnership with Mr Spicer in the mid-eighteenth century. On his death in 1777 his two daughters inherited his estate between them. One daughter had married Alderman John Carter who led the Corporation's struggle against the Admiralty in the eighteenth century for the right to nominate MPs for the borough. The other daughter had married John Bonham of Petersfield. Sir John Carter, son of the Alderman and grandson of William, took over the running of the business. His son, John, came into the Bonham share of William Pike's estate in 1826 and joined the name of Bonham to Carter. The brewery remained in the hands of the family until 1911 when it was incorporated into Brickwoods Ltd and this is probably why the group photograph of the employees was commissioned at this time.

(PCRO 1499A/27 and PCRO 694A/9/1/159)

Portsmouth had a number of mineral water factories in the late nineteenth and early twentieth centuries. Lyle's factory (above and below) stood on the corner of Cardiff Road and North End Avenue. (PCM 129/1991)

The committee of the Portsmouth Costermongers' Union, 1905. Trading in street markets has remained important until the present day, especially for foodstuffs. There has been a slow trend towards formalisation of shopping in shops, however, particularly for more expensive items. This banner is now in Portsmouth City Museums' collections.   (PCM 1231/1974)

R.J.Taylor traded in 1901 from addresses in Broad Street, Portsmouth, and at Kingston Cross. This shot was probably taken at Christmas time. Such 'festive' scenes were popular and the weather was cold enough not to damage the stock!

(PCRO 1433A/12/17)

Bishop Bros Boot and Shoe Maufacturers, nd, *c.*1900. James Bishop began manufacturing boots and shoes in Southampton in 1850. Ten years later he opened a shop at 198 Commerical Road, Portsmouth, and this became the main shop in the early 1890s. By 1900 there were branches in Gosport, Havant, Winchester and, for a while, London as well as other towns and cities. The actual manufacture of shoes ceased in 1905 but the firm continued in the family's possession, becoming a limited company only in 1949. There are premises today in Arundel Street, Portsmouth, and High Street, Gosport.
(PCRO 530A/3/5/2)

The Palmerston Grocery Stores, Tea and Italian Warehouse, *c.*1909. The firm traded at 77 Palmerston Road and did not go out of business until the late 1970s. It was known latterly as Whitcombs.
(PCRO 1075A)

Interior from a collection of photographs of draper Will Brown's London Road and Twyford Avenue premises, *c*.1930. Will Brown opened his first shop in Twyford Avenue *c*.1913-14 and, in 1930, new premises in London Road. The Twyford Avenue shop was closed in 1934 but the London Road premises expanded throughout the 1950s until they were eventually closed in the late 1960s.   (PCRO 348A/1/2/12)

William Waterman Junior, dairyman, had premises at 158 Highland Road, Southsea. This photograph was taken in Eastney Street before 1914.   (PCRO 801A/2/1)

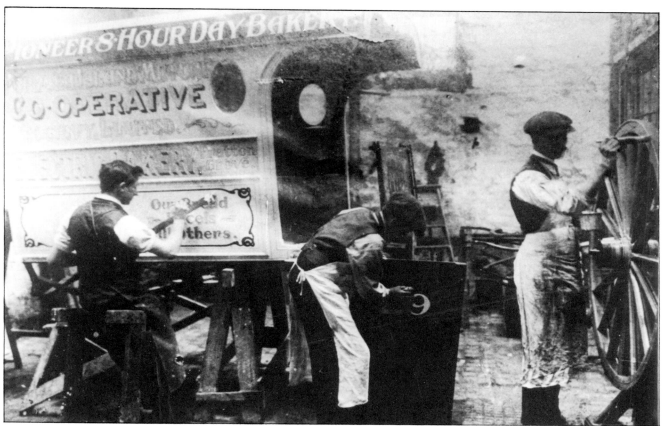

The paintshop of the Portsea Island Mutual Co-operative Society, about 1910. PIMCO was an important organisation with a large workforce. It delivered both bread and milk and maintained a big fleet of horse-drawn delivery wagons.

(PCM 17/1977)

Council workmen laying drainpipes, c.1900. One of the many tasks that local government took on in the nineteenth century was providing sewers and drains. These workmen have no mechanical help. They are reliant on their own strength, and that of their horse.

(PCM 463/1974)

Laying tramtracks in Twyford Avenue, between 1914 and 1920. The grooved rails in which the tramwheels ran are quite clear. Notice the flat caps of the workmen and the bowler and leggings of the official.   (PCM)

Group of Carr's Blackit Boot Polish salesmen with handcart outside the shop of F.Emery, Florist, Doner Terrace, Milton Road, at the corner of Velder Avenue, *c.*1930.
                                     (PCRO 801A/2/5)

Airspeed came to Portsmouth in 1933, the year after the corporation opened the airfield. The company went through some difficult patches but soon became an important local employer, with over 2,000 staff. It was taken over by De Havilland and closed during the 1960s.   (PCM 45p/1988)

Transport

The Southsea Carriage Co established *c.*1904 was to be found in Clarence Mews, Auckland Road East. In due course it became Jn Savage and Co Ltd's motor garage.   (PCRO 69A/2/1)

A horse-drawn bus of the type common in Portsmouth from about 1870 until 1919. The horses are painfully thin —
the animals pulling buses and trams seem rarely to have been well fed.   (PCM 1311/1974)

A rare picture of a horse-drawn charabanc, *c.*1910. It is turning north into Commercial Road opposite the *Central Hotel*,
on the corner of Edinburgh Road.   (PCM 103/1956/56b)

The firm of White and Co Ltd, Removal Contractors, was established in 1871. An agreement by which White and Co acted as carters for the Great Western Railway in Gosport and Portsmouth was drawn up in 1873. This photograph was taken *c.*1925.

(PCRO 971A/1/8/27)

While horse-drawn removal vans were adequate for general carrying, house removal required something like this Winchester iron-tyred Foden Steam Wagon and trailer with driver Stan Eldridge and steersman Albert Dunford, *c.*1922.

(PCRO 971A/1/8/29)

Horses and carts are the motive power at Colyer's yard, by Cosham Station, *c.*1900. The manager, Mr Peter Maybee, wears a bowler hat, his staff wear caps. Headgear marks out their status. Colyer's were general carriers and coal merchants.
(PCM H/66/92)

Thirty years later Mr Maybee's son Len and his colleague load a motor van in the station yard. The company closed not long after, a victim of the Depression.
(PCM H/66/92)

Guildhall Square in 1899. This is a rare picture of a Portsmouth single-deck horse-drawn tram. Such trams disappeared on the electrification of the system in 1901.   (PCM 966/1974d)

Horse-drawn trams in 1899. At this date the tramway system belonged to the Provincial Tramway Co. The photographer was standing on the corner of King's Terrace and Kings Road. Museum Road goes off to the left, Landport Terrace is behind the female pedestrian.   (PCM 966/1974a)

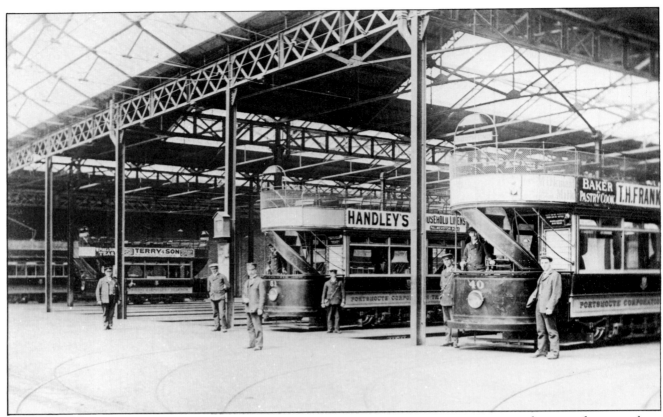

The tram depot in Gladys Avenue, North End, c.1905. The corporation bought the tramway system by compulsory purchase in 1901. Some of the trams were converted to electric traction (the museum owns one), but many new ones were bought.
(PCM)

The tram terminus, Cosham, c.1930. It was situated just south of the station, where the current bus terminus is.
(PCM 201/1981c)

Photographs on this and following page taken during the construction of the **Portsdown & Horndean Light Railway** by C.H.T.Marshall of London Road, Waterlooville, 1900. **(PCRO 372A/2/4, 6-7)**

A Portsdown & Horndean Light Railway car wends its way up Portsdown Hill. This photograph was taken before 1914 by Stephen Cribb, a well-known local photographer, of 61 St Andrew's Road, Southsea.   (PCRO 194A/3/2)

Dismantling the last trams to run in Portsmouth. The final journey, by four trams in procession, took place on 10 November 1936. The first electric tram service began on 19 September 1901.   (PCM 186/1976)

Trolley bus 24 picking up passengers at St Mary's church, 1934-8. The first trolley bus service ran on 4 August 1934. Trolley buses were more comfortable and quieter than trams; they also picked up their passengers from the curb, unlike trams, which were confined to the centre of the road by their rails so their passengers had to walk out into the roadway.

(PCM 135/1976)

A Karrier WL6 bus with a 60-seater body, built 1928, overtakes a horse and cart during floods on Copnor Road, Hilsea, about 1930.

(PCM 646/1945b)

Tower Garages, Castle Road, 1905. This photograph shows a number of early motor vehicles and a new twentieth-century craftsman, the motor mechanic. Many garages grew out of bicycle shops, while at least one local carriage builder, Hoads, dabbled in motor car manufacture in the early days of the industry. (PCM 474/1974)

The steam locomotive *Portsmouth*, nd. It was built for the LBSCR in 1864. (PCRO 121A/3/20)

Cosham Station from the footbridge, *c*.1900.   (PCM 200/1981)

Copnor crossing, at the corner of Kingston Cemetery, was replaced by the present road bridge about 1907.

(PCM 191/1956)

Portsmouth and Southsea Station was built in 1847 and operated jointly by the London, Brighton and South Coast Railway and the London and South Western Railway. They were amalgamated in 1923 as part of the Southern Railway. The high-level platforms were provided when the tracks were extended to the Hard in 1876. The goods yard was on the south side of the tracks, here (in 1934) wagons from at least two other companies can be seen. (PCM 732/1976)

The new harbour station at Portsmouth, 1876. In the background are the *Duke of Wellington, Victory, Himalaya* and the *St Vincent* training ship. (PCRO 1712A/1/1/1)

A branch line was built from Fratton Station to near South Parade Pier in 1884-5. It was closed in 1914. Its terminus, Southsea Station, had already become Baldwin Millard's Garage. The branch never generated enough traffic to be profitable, partly because it was quicker to reach the pier by tram from Portsmouth Station than to change at Fratton.

(PCM 469/1974)

The *Hilsea*, a car ferry on the Portsmouth-Fishbourne service, painted by W.A. Jeffries *c*.1960. The first ro-ro ferry on this route was introduced by the Southern Railway in 1927. *Hilsea* entered service in 1930 and was replaced by larger vessels in 1961.

(PCM 478/1970)

Pigs disembarking from the Isle of Wight car ferry at Point *c.*1950. Livestock was landed at Point and driven through the streets of Portsmouth until comparatively recently. Before the car ferries were introduced animals were towed across the Solent in open boats. (PCM 116/1986/2)

Brittany Ferries' new super ferry, *Normandie,* unloading at the Continental Ferry Port, summer 1992. The Ferry Port has established itself as second only to Dover in the number of passengers handled each year.　　(PCRO Reprogr.102/92/A9)

This photograph taken by photographer Reginald Silk *c.*1909 of the aviator Graham Gilmour shows Gilmour as he took off from the narrow roadway on the southern boundary of the Haslar Royal Naval Hospital and flew out to sea. It was on this occasion that he 'shelled' the submarine headquarters at Fort Blockhouse.　　(PCRO 1083A/1/2/35)

A hydroplane off Southsea beach by Stephen Cribb, *c*.1910.

(PCRO 813A/1/1)

A Channel Airways Douglas DC3 aircraft at Portsmouth Airport in the mid-1950s. At this point in its history, the airport, opened in 1932, began to show a profit. It became a regional airport and by the mid-1960s was handling 63,000 passengers a year. However with only grass runways it could not compete with other municipal airports and it eventually closed in 1973. The aircraft construction company Airspeed Ltd moved to Portsmouth Airport in 1932-3 and it was here that the first commercial aircraft with a retractable undercarriage to be produced in England was built and test flown by Flt.Lt. G.H.Stainforth.

(PCRO DL/P)

An SRN 6 hovercraft operated by Hovertravel Ltd at Clarence Pier. The company's first scheduled crossing from Southsea to Ryde was on 24 July 1965. This service is the descendant of the paddle-steamer ferries which originally operated from the pier. A watercolour by W.A.Jefferies, painted *c*.1966. (PCM 461/1970)

'Having a Good Time'

The ball given by the town of Portsmouth for the officers of the French squadron visiting Portsmouth in 1865. The middle classes were able to enjoy this sort of entertainment often during the nineteenth century — 'assembly rooms' such as the King's Rooms were actually ballrooms. This ball was on a particularly lavish scale. (PCM)

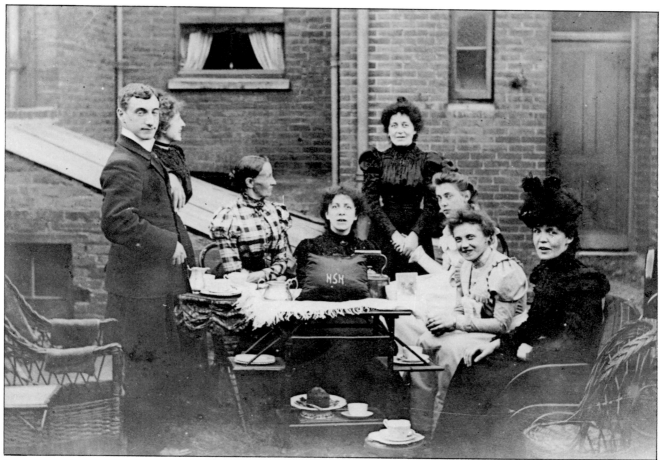

A tea party in the back yard of a terraced house in 1899. A more modest way of enjoying yourself! These people were not poor, but they were far from rich. Puffed shoulders were clearly in fashion, while before 1918 adult women almost always wore their hair long but gathered into a bun.   (PCM 1004/1974d)

Edwardian summer crowds in Pier Road, c.1903, mostly visiting the Hippodrome and Menagerie belonging to Lord John Sanger & Sons. Circuses were popular throughout the nineteenth and early twentieth centuries and permanent buildings were provided to house them, as well as the traditional big top. Despite the warmth of a sunny day all but a few of the strollers wear hats. The women are tightly corseted, while the men wear jackets and ties. Everyone dressed 'up', i.e. formally, to enjoy themselves.
                                                                                                                                    (PCM)

Sanger's circus elephants bathing in the sea off the Clarence Esplanade, 1899. Animals were not only used in circuses, but even elephants appeared on stage in theatres and music halls.   (PCM 963/1974d)

Women and children on Southsea beach, pre-1914.   (PCRO 801A/2/7)

The diving platform of the Ladies Section of the Portsmouth Swimming Club, c.1912. The swimmers are decently attired in long bathing costumes and are shielded from public view while on the platform by canvas screens. Nevertheless, what a sense of freedom bathing costumes must have given compared with the corsets, long skirts, voluminous petticoats and big hats which women usually wore!   (PCM 646/1945h)

Members of Portsmouth Swimming Club sunbathing on Southsea Beach, 1938. The club was founded in 1875 and once boasted over 1,700 members. Sunbathing was introduced from the USA in the 1920s. Before then tanned skin was thought ugly and indicated you were working class. Women carried parasols to protect their faces. Swimming costumes naturally became smaller. Public morality also became more relaxed — mixed bathing was not allowed in Portsmouth before 1911.

(PCM 152/1976)

Bathing Belles, Southsea, nd.

(PCRO DL/P)

Miss Rose Taplin, Portsmouth's May Queen, descends the steps of the Town Hall on May Day, 1910. She is about to get into a motor car which will carry her in a procession around the town. The size of the crowd shows how popular was celebrating this traditional holiday in the Edwardian period. There were also elaborate ceremonies in Wymering in the nineteenth century.

(PCM 653/1945e)

Guides in Camp, 'Northlands', 1924.   (PCRO 838A/1/2)

North End Cycling Club on an outing, c.1905. Cycling was at first a rich man's sport, but by this date bicycles were inexpensive enough to be far more widely enjoyed. Most of these riders wear suits and ties — there were few leisure clothes.

(PCM 305/1980)

A field day for local sea scouts north of Portsdown Hill, June 1911. (PCRO 224A/1/1/20-7-8)

The fair on the slopes of Portsdown Hill, photographed on a bank holiday Monday c.1905. Fort Widley looms on the skyline.

was built on the original site of the August fair. Portsdown Hill fair was authorised by letters patent in 1715.   (PCM H5.3)

A street tea party to celebrate the coronation of George V, in Emanuel Street, Landport, in 1935. It was organised b

Mrs Teadham. Such tea parties were a real treat for poorer children.   (PCM 354/1981)

Donkey rides on Portsdown Hill one bank holiday before 1906. The hill was a favourite spot for outings, especially after the tramway from Portsmouth was built. (PCM H5.3)

Bowls has long been a popular sport and eighteenth-century bowls have been found by the museum's archaeologists on a site in Old Portsmouth. This is one of the corporation's greens on Southsea Common, photographed in 1938. (PCM 151/1976)